Resilie

Reflections From a  *...ary*

Barbara Mahama

Table of Contents

Dedication i

Special Acknowledgement ii

About the Author v

A Heavenly Call 1

Memories Shared 11

A Kind Man 18

Saying Goodbye 22

Culture/Perceptions/Projections/Expectations 29

This Is Where We Are 36

Lessons 38

Grace 40

Knowing Me 41

Reality Of The Loss 56

Independence 63

Days like These 68

Finding Courage to Press On and Move Forward 103

God Sends Help 106

Caution 109

While Waiting 110

A Child's Emotions 113

Single Parenting 117

Spiritual Battles 124

Highlights of Years Three To Five 126

Emails from Admirers..137

Time Wasters 155

Letters to Daddy..156

Some Words of Exhortation from the Bible 158

Dedication

For Jaden and Jerry

Mummy has grown wings enough to teach you how to fly and if I have to grow new wings every day, I will. Maybe this whole tragedy is about you and the purpose you carry. This is a promise to you; I will hold your hands to direct you, with the help of God, to enable you to walk into that purpose fully. Your destinies shall not be cut off. You will be a force to contend with.

Love: Your mum, life coach, pastor, prophetess, cook, chauffeur, nurse, friend, gisting partner, tour guide...we are in this together, and we are all we have, so we have to make it work!

For Maxwell Adam Mahama

Thank you for loving me and sharing your short life with me. I am indeed grateful you had confidence in me to hold the fort in your absence. We love you, and we miss you!

Special Acknowledgement

The journey has been ruthless and tough, but I have enjoyed a lot of blessings hence a need to show appreciation;

- ➢ I am grateful for the opportunity to work throughout this journey, giving me some sort of escape and something to occupy my mind with and definitely a regular income.
- ➢ I am ever grateful for the role my in-laws played in my marital life; the help, the friendship, and the love.
- ➢ Ghanaians showed so much love and care. Your prayers were felt and made an impact. I gained friends and family from people who used to be strangers. Thank you!
- ➢ Thank you to my family, friends, and church who stood with me and continue to do so. God will reward you.
- ➢ The privilege of channeling my love and energy to nurture my two wonderful boys. I see Maxwell in them like I've never seen before. Loving and caring for them is such a pleasure. It's like Maxwell never went away.

➢ Finally, to a loving God who has shown so much trust in me that I can handle this predicament and the consequences thereafter.

Isaiah 43:2 New International Version (NIV)

2. When you pass through the waters,

I will be with you;

and when you pass through the rivers,

they will not sweep over you.

When you walk through the fire,

you will not be burned;

the flames will not set you ablaze.

About the Author

Barbara Mahama is a young Ghanaian lady who has risen above the pain of losing a husband in the cruelest and most barbaric of ways and has carved a path of success for herself and her children. She is the epitome of strength, grace, and resilience.

A Heavenly Call

As the media space got flooded with news of a 'supposed armed robber' that had been burnt, I was caught up in my own little world, working through my normal daily routine.

On 29th May 2017, I had passed through UNDP Ghana to see my boss, and when I was about to leave, he was reading something on the internet about an armed robber being burnt. I was not interested in going close to see the burnt body or even reading the story because sad stories have a way of spoiling my mood. To be frank, I was preoccupied with the fact that I had not heard from Maxwell for the greater part of the day and was very worried about the WhatsApp messages I had sent that showed a single tick. Little did I know that the story my boss was reading was about my husband, and little did I know that my life was about to change drastically.

Back in the car, I kept calling Maxwell's mobile number, but it was off. I went to the kids' school and picked them up. I was worried but tried hard to tell myself I would hear from him. I passed the market with the kids to get them bananas, knowing they liked it and because Maxwell would be happy to hear the kids tell him, "Mummy bought banana."

I sent the final logo of a sewing business we were planning to do to Maxwell, and that also got one tick. I also sent a picture I took of the kids that morning, knowing those pictures kept him going, but he didn't even get to see the last picture of Jaden helping Jerry do his homework.

Neighbours were checking on me and asking for my pastor's number, which felt weird, but I still kept a cool head. I told one Lt. Col, who was then a Major, of my inability to reach Maxwell and requested for the number of any person who was at the post with him at the village. He said he did not have any number to reach Maxwell on. Prior to my asking him for the number, he had come to check on us to ask whether we were fine. He knew!

My father-in-law was also called, and the fear became great, so I was just waiting to see what all the weird pieces would lead to. My father-in-law called my father to meet him in Burma Camp (Military barracks in Accra, Ghana), where we lived. Subsequently, I was called by my father, whose head was in the clouds too. The confusion was too much. My father wanted to know what the problem was, and I told him I had no idea except I had not heard from Maxwell since morning. I called my father-in-law to ask him whether he had heard from Maxwell throughout the day, and he said no. We spoke about the last time we all heard from him.

I was now getting apprehensive, especially as I received a few strange text messages asking me whether the news circulating was true or not. I did not know about any news circulating. I just wanted to maintain a calm composure because I was already exhausted from putting together all the strange signals I was picking up. For some strange reason, I had no time to be on Facebook that very day, as I was engrossed in planning for the business that Maxwell and I had planned to set up. I don't know if I could have handled the shock of whatever was circulating that very moment, and I am grateful to God that He kept me from seeing them. My pastor came over around 6 pm after a neighbour called him to come to my house. I have never been able to ask him whether he knew of the story before coming. I think I prefer to leave it that way. He later took my phone from me so I would not be disturbed by the strange messages I was getting. My father came in later and said he was with my father-in-law at the officers' mess, and I said okay.

After the meeting at the officers' mess, my father-in-law and my father led a military delegation to my place around 7:30 pm to tell me my husband was involved in an accident and he was in a critical condition. They told me that the doctors were doing their best to control the situation. I looked at them and said okay, and they left, leaving my father-in-law, father, and pastor. The delegation looked shattered when they broke the news to me. I can imagine how difficult it was for them to put up a brave face. I can imagine the discussions they had before entering the room. I can even imagine the various scenarios they played in their individual minds concerning my possible reaction. When they left, I asked my father-in-law whether Maxwell was in a military vehicle, and he said yes. He himself looked too lost. Somehow, I felt the news was worse than what they made me believe, but I had to ask him the questions because I didn't want the situation whereby I would hear that he wasn't on official duties, as the consequences of finding oneself in a wrong place with a uniform can be unpleasant.

I pictured Maxwell involved in an accident and in a critical condition. A lot of thoughts rushed through my mind; was the driver speeding? How can an accident in such a village put someone in a critical condition? That fateful Monday night, I was picturing his body in pieces from the accident but still seeing the pieces coming back together to make him whole and come back to us the way he went. After everyone went away to prepare for the next day, I was left with my pastor and the kids. Ceaseless prayers went up that night. I had my playlist also, and I was soaking inspirational songs.

My pastor urged me to sleep, but how could I? My sleep was full of wincing as if I was in pain, "mmh," was all I was saying till he called me to ask what was wrong, and I said I couldn't sleep. I will never be able to accurately explain to anyone how I felt that night because it was the first time I felt that way. I felt sick in my stomach, and my heart felt like someone's hand was in my chest, ripping it apart. I felt nauseous, too, and attempted vomiting at one point. The kids woke up at dawn with no intention of sleeping again. They looked restless and confused. The atmosphere was different, understandably so; the head of the house had died, and although we did not know yet, every one of us was getting signals. There is an unexplainable spiritual connection between us and those we love.

I entirely abandoned the idea of sleep and attended to the kids. Looking back, I feel they had questions in their minds. The atmosphere was not the same for them. I got them ready for school in the morning. An in-law in the army offered to drop them off for me. I looked at them in utter dejection as they followed her. I realised that there was the possibility of unpleasant news coming in about their father in their absence.

We waited for the delegation again on 30th May 2017. They came and said Maxwell did not survive the accident and that he had died. Plans were underway to bring his body to Accra. I just looked at them and shook my head, saying okay in my head; tears had welled up, but I fought them back. I was finding it difficult to assimilate the message. It all sounded strange. Everything did not add up at all. I had no further questions to ask anyone. I didn't have the energy to probe. I just wanted to bury myself in the songs I had on my playlist. I just wanted to feel God's arms around me. In the moments where words fail us, our God is attentive to hear the questions our heartbeat asks Him.

I loved Maxwell with my whole mind, whole soul, whole body, and whole spirit. He was a good man, and he didn't deserve a half-hearted devotion. The verse in Colossians 3:23 states that "Whatever you do, work at it with all your heart, as working for the Lord, not for human masters"; I took it personally and loved him like I was loving God.

I couldn't help but recollect how the morning of the previous day had gone, especially the few moments we shared early in the morning on that Monday. I woke up a normal person with the day's activities lined up. I had agreed with my husband in April 2017 to end my various internships and be at home for a while. I struggled to get a job after my master's course. It was a real struggle, I got a few interviews, but that was all. I decided to take up various internships, especially with international organisations, and I am glad I did.

That fateful morning, we spoke very early, as usual, because he likes to know what I have planned for the day. For some reason, I had a lot to say, and I was unwilling to end our conversation, so he joked and said, "Can't a man use the loo in peace anymore?" This joking remark got us laughing. He had suffered from food poisoning a few days back, so he being able to create that humor gave me some kind of relief; I knew he was feeling much better.

I had a lot to update him on because of our sewing project. Maxwell gave attention to details, so I was prepared to furnish him with every piece of information he needed; choice of fabric, logo, threads, and many other things.

He said he would bathe and call me back, but the call never came. I got the kids ready, and I dropped them at school with the reality that they had a father who was away working in a village.

I went to the VRA clubhouse in Cantonments to use the free internet to research into few issues of interest. I then sent a message to my late husband, but I saw only one tick which meant the message wasn't delivered, and it was strange. I wanted to find out what he had for breakfast. I never knew what had happened then. I kept on trying to get in touch with him.

The closest the news of his gruesome murder could have gotten to me during the day's activities was when I passed through UNDP, but even then, I never thought in my wildest dreams that it could have been Maxwell. I recollect and begin to shudder, wondering what went wrong. Didn't I pray enough? Didn't I have raw faith? A child's faith? Didn't I stretch my faith far enough to believe that Maxwell could live again? God just had to know how much love I had for the man that held me in high esteem and always told me my future was bright. He once told me, "God didn't let you marry a rich man, but He made you marry a man who will push you to become a rich woman." I remember that two weeks before Maxwell died, I taught my Sunday school children how to be good Christians from one of Bishop Dag's books. I told the kids that a strong Christian isn't moved by the circumstances of life because their roots are strong in God.

The day Maxwell was nominated for that assignment, we sat down and had discussions about his going, his time away, and uncertainties, and prayed for the best. As dramatic as he was, he called Jaden to tell him he was embarking on a journey and was putting him in charge of the house and taking care of me. Playing back to the day he set off for the journey, he came back home while I was away to release an animal he had caught in the bush and kept in a cage. He spared the life of an animal, but his own life was never spared. All through the journey, we were communicating; I knew when they got to junction A or B, I even notified him of an explosion that had occurred ahead of them. He went and came back in a coffin…

Heartfelt Prayer to God

I am not attempting to understand why this happened.

You know me, you know my heart, and you formed me.

You knew me when I was just a clot of blood in my mother's womb.

You know what would break me and what wouldn't break me.

You said you know the plans you have for me, plans to prosper and not to harm me.

If I want to use my human mind, I would say your plans are harming me; your plans are causing me pain.

But I am taking your Word as it is, and I believe that your plans are that of good and not evil.

This world is full of pain, full of evil, full of selfishness, greed, and self-centeredness, and you have given human beings free will, trusting them to choose the right path, but that doesn't always happen.

The tears that fall from my face, you see them and the number of times they fall, you know.

The ones that don't fall but stay in the ducts, you also see.

Shine your face on me and give me rest, I am heavy laden.

Your yoke is light, so I prefer that one. Restore me, oh God. Lift up my head.

Memories Shared

I never thought of losing Maxwell in the manner it happened. This was supposed to be a forever journey; growing old together, seeing our children grow to fulfill their dreams, and seeing our grandchildren born. This sudden loss could break any heart as goodbyes could not be said to each other in the manner we best knew how. All I have are the memories we created together.

My first stop down memory lane has to do with how the spiritual journey we shared began. I never forced Maxwell to church; I always made him understand the importance of church. The Bible entreats us not to forsake the gathering of the brethren. I always said to him that to me, going to church was important, especially as baby Christians, because we spend the whole week out of the church, and there is nothing wrong in putting one day aside to go to church-iron sharpeneth iron. It is wonderful how COVID-19 has now made it possible for us to join prayer meetings all through the day online.

Maxwell decided to go to the Catholic Church in Burma Camp more often because he was baptised in the Catholic Church. There was a time he left his tithe card with me, and

I made payments twice in his absence while he was on a peacekeeping mission.

I didn't force him to follow me to my church; One day, he decided to join me in my church permanently. He always sat at the back, and he was nice to everyone. He decided to engage more because I took part in church duties after the close of service. He willingly took it upon himself to be engaging the young men, chatting with them after church while I did what I was supposed to do.

Sundays after church always had a great feeling. We bonded deeper as a family as we engaged in one activity or the other when we got home and later settled to eat and prepare for the week; that was our Sunday routine.

There were times he even went for programmes without me, especially while I was heavily pregnant with Jerry. He usually returned with excitement, sharing with me what was preached. We were open-minded; I never forced any suggestion down his throat. Maxwell was someone you couldn't force anything down his throat, he would analyse, and if he felt your path was the right one, he would let you know, and if it wasn't, he would not mince words at all. I always told him he had a sharp mouth.

The church attendance momentum he gained dwindled because there was always something to do; the military career wasn't an easy one.

When I met him, he had no prayer life (he said so himself). I never forced him to pray. I just went ahead and prayed for all of us audibly. He saw me waking up at dawn to pray and read my Bible, so he just started waking up also to read his Bible. Then later, it became a daily morning routine that we did together to the extent that he started leading devotions.

We grew, and progressed as a young family on a journey to making life meaningful for us. On Jaden's 2nd birthday, I wasn't with them, but he excitedly reported on how he prayed fervently at his dad's end. His dad, who was marveled, asked rhetorically who the pastor was; him or me? I was pleased to hear that.

He moved from a prayerless life to answered prayers life. When Jerry was some months old, Maxwell had a dream. Maxwell wasn't a dreamer, so he was surprised I always had one dream after the other, but he also started having dreams and remembering them. He dreamt that Jerry had fallen from his cot and had developed into a critical condition. He didn't like the dream and hence put it into prayer. He told me about it when I woke up and admonished me that we had to watch Jerry well to avoid falls.

The following day, I went out and entered the room just in time to realise that if I hadn't entered at that time, Jerry would have fallen from his cot. Prayers lead to dreams, and dreams are revelations. I will never take any credit because when God chooses someone, He gives the person grace. I am just glad that I was there and saw how Maxwell went through various spiritual stages. I understand that as humans, we keep growing, evolving, learning, and going through various spiritual growth processes because, first of all, we are spirit beings, and our father in heaven desires to connect with us.

I realised that there seemed to be recurring disturbing dream patterns over a period of time. We sought God's face during those times, believing that God would avert any of the predicaments that the dreams seemed to suggest.

Samples of those dreams are below:

1. The tree falling on Maxwell: When Jerry was about three months old in 2015, Maxwell was on a peacekeeping mission. I dreamt there was a heavy downpour that uprooted a big Nim tree behind where we lived. I went out to look at the tree that had fallen, and I saw Maxwell under it, hurt, so I helped him come out from under the tree. I woke up and asked myself what kind of dream that was. I felt heavy and

uncomfortable and prayed that whole week, sending him specific verses to pray with. He came home not long after that dream with a problem; he was repatriated, and he was banned from traveling. We decided to look at the brighter side of everything and consoled ourselves with the fact that he would be around to see Jerry celebrate his first birthday, and we thanked God for life. However, later, we realised a need to intensify our prayers concerning certain issues.

2. The water overflow: On 10th May 2017, I penned down instances of having dreams of gushing water, destroying things, and coming towards me. Maxwell had left for an anti-galamsey operation (an exercise to halt illegal mining in some parts of the country). Jerry had celebrated his 2nd birthday on 4th May. In the dreams, the sea spilled over, coming towards our settlement with speed, carrying things and people along, and it always stopped at my feet, which I didn't understand. Out of the lot, one which I deemed serious was when I saw myself hiding in a room with my little brother. Looking at the speed of the water, I knew it would cover our heads, and we would drown. I looked at the gushing water and closed my eyes, believing that was the end of me; I said, "Unto thy hands, I commit my spirit, God." By that utterance, the water stopped at the room we were hiding in. I still don't understand those dreams. I

prayed fervently and for long, asking God to take control. I could dream, and there would be heavy downpours with serious thunder and chaos everywhere except where I stood at that particular time in the dream. All I can say is that, in the midst of the storm, there was peace around me.

3. The spell confirming his dream: In this dream, maybe in March or April 2017, I heard a knock on our bedroom door, and I wondered how the person entered the first door to get to the second door, which is the bedroom door. Maxwell opened it, I didn't see who was there, but the person sprinkled something on Maxwell and went away. All I saw was that Maxwell was falling backwards, so I rushed out to go and see who did that only to realise that the person, a man, had reached the last end of the road towards a bush. I shouted at the person to come back whilst questioning him on what he did to my husband. I don't know why the man looked shocked that I could shout and call him to come back, but he came back, and I started praying and cancelling whatever he did. It looked like a challenge between the man and me. I was victorious in the end; he vanished, and I went inside. I spoke in tongues in the dream, praying fervently hence waking up tired. Admittedly, I was not enthused by the dream, so I called Maxwell and told him we needed to intensify our prayers because I dreamt someone entered our

room and sprinkled a spell or something on him, and he immediately remembered his dream that was a bit similar to mine.

He said he dreamt that he saw a group of people who looked like they were chanting, and he told God to give him the power to challenge and defeat them. He said he started praying, and all of a sudden, the ground opened, and the people entered one by one. He said to himself that he was surprised he could triumph over them and was equally surprised that there were people who could do such weird stuff. We prayed together after he narrated his dream.

A Kind Man

The name Maxwell Adam Mahama has been on the lips of many, especially after the world witnessed his gruesome murder. He had many sides and many dreams. Sometimes, a man's dreams and aspirations help you to truly know who he is or was. He was a kind man with a good heart towards others. He cared deeply.

One of the caretakers at the military cemetery in Osu, Accra, recounted how Maxwell helped him when he fell into trouble years back. I said to myself, "That was who Maxwell was, ever ready to offer help." He had a good heart. Maxwell was ever ready to help the wives of the officers who were on peacekeeping missions. He was there when their cars had issues, he was there when a child needed to be rushed to the hospital, and he was there when a door needed to be broken because he had every tool you could think of. He was the man with the wildest and unthinkable fun dreams. He wanted to walk to Tamale and back and make a documentary out of that experience or go on a safari somewhere far away in his pickup, stopping in the night to hunt; very adventurous indeed! He actually saw himself as an actor and movie producer later in his life. He was a movie lover and could stay up late into the night watching movies. We joked that he had to be a movie producer and actor in the near future because all the time he spent watching movies had to bring some benefit.

The pet lover, the humorist (he wanted to do stand-up comedy one day), the analyser, and the sports lover. He was a good swimmer and a lover of tennis, and he started playing golf. He loved to develop himself and was resolute in acquiring knowledge hence combining his MSC with an MBA and French and even wanted to add Law. We supported each other's dreams. He was intelligent, hardworking, very neat, and playful but serious in life. I have good memories of his assignment deadlines because we had in-depth discussions about his topics. I particularly found the MBA topics interesting, but he didn't live to finish that course, a course we agreed would put a strain on his finances, but it was worth the try.

Maxwell was generous; his Ford pickup was accessible to all his close friends in Burma Camp who needed to move heavy items around. The church even became a beneficiary of such benevolence on his path as the pickup was released for occasions where chairs needed to be moved for programmes. He was ever ready to help, and he helped. There were instances when he was out of the country, and a friend's mother needed money, and he would tell me to send the money that was needed. I never stopped him from extending help because I trusted him to make good decisions. I never stopped him from extending help because never did I feel that he should be available only to his wife and kids. Maxwell was free to be Maxwell.

He was a good husband, a good father, a good son, a planner, and a goal achiever. He could sit and plan our future home with different species of dogs, birds, and all sorts of exciting things. He even started making a boat, and on such days, you would hear lectures on outboard motors and whatnot. There was never a dull moment with Maxwell. Neighbours were always interested in what his next project would be. From bird rearing to lettuce and carrot farming to catching snakes, he lived. He was a lover of life! He was full of life! He had plans for his sons, good plans…

Memories, more memories all rushing in, including those of the few days I had with my husband before his demise. Thursday, 25th May 2017, I will never forget that day. I woke up, dropped the kids at school, parked the car at their school, walked to the junction, and picked public transport (trotro) to church. Anytime my husband was away, I tried to reduce expenditure in every way possible. While in the "trotro", I had a chat with him, he asked how the day was going, and I told him everything was fine. I recounted what

I had done so far for the morning, including my journey to the church. He wondered why I would not stay home and pray, but I explained that there were some prayer topics that would never occur to me to pray when I prayed alone.

I got to church with the mind to pray. As we were exhorted to pray, I prayed with all fervency as if I knew my life depended on it. I am not sure I followed the prayer topics well. I prayed for my husband, he had always been my prayer topic, but this time, it was as if I knew something was about to happen. I remember saying that I take his soul out of the pit of hell (I think I paused to ask myself why I said that, and I told myself that hell was any difficult or nasty situation). There were many nasty situations going on at that time, especially with regard to his career. I prayed that it would be well with him and he would succeed in every aspect of his life. I knew the future was bright for us. I had so much faith in him and what he wanted to achieve in life. My hopes and dreams were shattered…

Saying Goodbye

When death comes too close to home,

Be still and know that I am God!

When life hits you too hard,

Be still and know that I am God!

When it all seems so confusing, and there is darkness all around,

Be still and know that I am God

My loss made me realise how much we should all prepare for death though we know subconsciously that we should. When people far from you die, you sympathise with their families; you even shed some tears depending on the circumstances that led to the death or the age of the person. You never imagine it will happen to you anytime soon, and when it finally happens, confusion sets in, anger sets in, and emotions are unstable, but finally, any fear of death just fades off. Sometimes, you don't mind dying also because, after all, the person who just passed was so close to you, your lives were intertwined, and you never thought you could be separated in such an abrupt manner. Finally, you console yourself with the fact that your loved one is in a new place, maybe in the next room where you can't be at the moment because you haven't reached that stage yet. You come to understand that life is indeed a stage, and we have all come to perform our roles, and when the cue is over, you exit, but when you exit, your co-actors are on the stage performing their parts, and finally, you all come back and bow. I have concluded that we never lose our loved ones. They are very close to us.

Death makes you appreciate what transitioning is all about. It makes you thankful for the dawn of every morning as you have another opportunity to prepare well. How is it that you gladly enjoy the grace of God and yet criticise your neighbour for enjoying that same grace? No human being decides whom God's grace should locate or otherwise. Never play God!

When news of a death is broken, there is massive mobilisation from all angles. You see family members you hardly see and in-laws you've never seen. Friends from primary school start appearing. That is how it is, and that time isn't the time to question why family member A wasn't at the marriage ceremony but has all of a sudden made appearance. According to Ecclesiastes 7:2, It is better to go to a house of mourning than to go to a house of feasting, for death is the destiny of everyone; the living should take this to heart. My pastor was there when the news was broken, and most of our branch members lived inside Burma Camp, El-Wak, and nearby. People had started trooping into the house by late morning on 30th May, and I needed to sit outside so they could offer their condolences. Neighbours helped me look for a black skirt and top I had thrown somewhere. Two ladies from my church had to rush to find black cloth to sew straight dresses for me, and by evening, they had brought them with scarves and slippers. The 5BN unit had started setting up canopies, and chairs were brought in. At a point when more chairs were needed, I saw some members of my church bringing chairs they rent out in pickups other than Maxwell's own. The following days were routinely torturous as I had to sit outside for people to come. The enormity of the issue, which was oblivious to the immediate family, even made the crowd that trooped in more confusing. The presence of the media even made it worse. From the little conversations that went around, I understood the seriousness of the situation. Maxwell hadn't died in an accident. I heard things like he didn't deserve what they did to him. My room which was always almost empty prior to the event, was now filled with family and friends who were busy serving guests. In-laws brought food, and at a point, food needed to be provided for those who were fasting for

Ramadan at the time to break their fast in the evenings. A counsellor was brought in by the military to try and help me manage the shock of death. We had chatting sessions, and we talked about general issues and God.

One afternoon, during a nap, after the visitors had reduced a bit, I heard two of my friends playing Joe Mettle's "Owanwani", and the song moved me in my dreams, so I insisted they kept playing that song over and over again. One of my friends took it upon herself to make sure Joe Mettle came to visit me during that time, so she looked for his number to try and arrange for a visit.

The burial date was slated for 9th June 2017. A vigil was held a day before the burial, and Joe Mettle's song was played because he had traveled and couldn't be at the burial. I walked to the vigil grounds, seeing all the crowd and all the media houses, Maxwell was dead, and a vigil was being held. I remembered the days he was part of funeral committees for his unit, and he had to be part of the organisation, meeting families and settling issues. This life!

The Burial

He was brought to the house early in the morning. There were tears and mention of his name. People were asking why amidst tears. I stood by the coffin and looked at it, and I imagined him whole and vibrant. I imagined his smiling face; he was so full of life. The feeling that someone went somewhere whole and came in a casket isn't a nice feeling. He left the house healthy and alive and came back dead. When a situation is new to me, I like to stay calm and see what will happen next. We headed to the State House for the burial service and went to the Osu Military cemetery to bury him.

I had pictures in my mind. Pictures of Maxwell waiting for me in front of our block anytime I went out with his pickup, which was manually operated. He was just too excited that his wife could drive a manual pickup and move around freely with it; he would shout and laugh, and "flow" me and say, "B! That's my wife!" He always said he wanted me to be independent and tough when he was not around.

I knew he would be cheering me on, and I was not ready to bow my head in any way because I felt the devil would be winning. When the devil touched Job's possessions and children, he knew he was touching something precious that had the ability to cripple him forever. The devil failed with Job, and he had to know that he was failing again with me. I wrote my own tribute within the shortest possible time, and I knew I wanted to read it myself. I wrote a letter to my king, and I wanted to read it myself, so I did. He knew he married a capable woman, and I was not ready to disappoint him in any way. It never occurred to me that someone would want to read my tribute for me, so I later found it odd that people were complaining about me reading my own written tribute.

Frankly, I felt it was no big deal. I felt it was normal, but it didn't mean I felt less pain. Truthfully speaking, the walk to the podium to read the tribute was the longest walk I had taken although it was a short distance. After the burial, the confusion continued as people expected me to behave a certain way, but I didn't meet their expectations. Little did they know that I was in my own world; I was visualizing how a life without Maxwell would be. Too many questions. Will the boys ever be okay without their father? How will they feel growing up and knowing how their father died? At this point, I knew the story; four or five days after the incident, one of my bishops, who was always around, asked me whether I wanted to see the pictures, and I said yes. He showed them to me, and he asked how I felt, so I told him that Maxwell was more than a piece of flesh, that the real Maxwell was not the one in the pictures. The real Maxwell is full of life; he is a spirit. He said yes, and added that there was a video of the incident, but he wouldn't want me to see it, and I agreed and told him I didn't want to see it. My mind was constantly occupied. I was confusingly in my own world while trying to stay sane.

Our journey to Maxwell's hometown to perform the other rights saw us in Bole through Wa to Tumu. I said to myself that the circumstances under which I was visiting should have been different.

Culture/Perceptions/Projections/Expectations

It is amazing how words get around quickly. It is also amazing how in mourning, people around you decide to peddle lies. It didn't take long for me to hear that I didn't mourn Maxwell enough. It is ridiculous for anyone to tell me I didn't mourn. I'm still mourning, and I will mourn for a long time.

I see the boys, and I see Maxwell. They talk, and I hear Maxwell; they walk, and I see Maxwell walking. So yes, sometimes I cry, sometimes I laugh, and that's my mourning, and it's enough.

For the rest of my life, I would be mourning Maxwell but on my own terms! What better way to show Maxwell that I loved him (not that he was ignorant of it) than to take excellent care of the kids he loved with every fiber of his soul? They said I didn't cry, but I leave that judgement to those who were really close to me, those who slept in the same room with me, those who called to pray with me on the phone, and I constantly broke down. Those who saw me waking up at dawn to type on my laptop while stifling tears so I wouldn't wake them up. People who called and realised I was crying and had to speak with friends around to go on walks with me for fresh air later turned around to tell me that I didn't even cry when Maxwell died.

In the midst of all the accusations and counter-accusations, I began to wonder where I was flawed or whether I didn't know much about our culture and traditions. I was enlightened to what the dictates of our culture expected of a widow then I realised how repressive the culture is. Repressive culture, in my opinion, is the culture that does not allow a wife to mourn her husband in a way she feels comfortable with. It is full of rules; You can't do this, you can't do that, you can't smile, you can't laugh, you can't live, and you can't surround yourself with the people you feel comfortable with. In a repressive culture, a widow's opinion doesn't matter.

The "Litmus test" in determining whether the cultural underpinnings of the society are repressive is to check how their widows are treated. A society that is comfortable dragging a widow to court to fight for properties her husband left. It's all around us. Finger-pointing and incessant accusations on widows; the commonest among such is the murder accusation. If your husband didn't die in your arms, chances are that you spiritually worked out your own husband's death.

Who makes a culture? Are you fueling negative culture? Do you find yourself saying, "This is how it is done here, so you have to do the same," even when it means someone's life is being snuffed out of her/him? Do you find yourself saying, "Oh, you are the child so overlook it?" If the way of life of the people around you does not contribute to your sanity, separate yourself and walk away with your head high. I define my culture...

Sometimes, your own pain is downgraded because of the position you find yourself in. When a woman loses her husband, the fact that another man may come her way sooner or later doesn't mean that she is a stone and can't feel pain. Another man may come, but it will not wipe away the years she shared with the man she lost. She went into the marriage, seeing herself growing old with the man she married. It is ridiculous to hear a day after your husband is buried, "Oh! She's young and will move on."

When my husband died, I lost my love, the father of my children, my friend and confidant, my better half, my fitness instructor, my head, my hero, my motivator, and my comedian. Additionally, I lost my ideas machine, my number one fan, my smile, and my dreams because when you spend years of your life planning and building for the future and your co-planner and co-builder is all of a sudden no more, it's painful! Now, that's a lot of losses, so don't go about downgrading a widow's pain. It is wrong to have the notion that a widow doesn't feel the pain of her loss because she can decide to get herself a man the next day her husband dies or because you think she is not the conventional widow, especially in her expression of grief.

Life is not always full of pleasantries, especially when we live with other people and perceptions exist. During mourning, you will hear hurtful things, things that can break you. For me, I heard that I am a possessive person, and as such, my marriage was bound to fail even if Maxwell hadn't died. To the best of my knowledge, I did my best as a wife committed to the call; I have helped my husband through the most difficult phase in his career. I stood by him even when he didn't see hope. I had faith when his faith was down. I was his song, his sunshine. I spoke life into him. My attitude of 'nothing is a big deal' helped us because two people cannot feel hopeless and helpless at the same time. When a negative comment came from his junior colleagues reminding him of his predicament, and he wanted to despair, my ears were ever ready to listen and to assuage his fears of the worst. When he wanted to break down because he felt a negative report that would destroy his career had been written about him, I was there to ask him, "Whose report will you believe?"

I also heard that I'm all about money. To put it appropriately, it was said, "I've seen money, so I've grown wings." Also, I heard that the only time I cried was when a discussion about money was held. I was even accused of opening a donation box, taking all the money out, closing the box, and saying there was no money in it. What people don't know is that there were times Maxwell got angry when I refused to buy anything for myself. I didn't like touching his money. I never pressured him to do things for me that would inconvenience him. I was too frugal. Even before we got married, he always left his ATM card with me before he went on peacekeeping missions, and he always came back to meet his money intact; we never had money fights. I didn't enter the marriage with an ulterior motive to hoard wealth and send it back home to better the lot of my family. For me, home was where my husband and children were, and everything centered on us. That is my only crime.

I must admit that I didn't grow up with a silver spoon in my mouth, and in fact, there were times we had no food to eat, but we grew up with contentment and were trained to not take things that belonged to others. I have been reminded time without a number of instances where I've had nothing to my name, implying that now that my husband is dead, I have a name. Even at your lowest, people will always want to put you in a box, and when you refuse to fit in the box, they will throw things at you and make you feel less of yourself. Rise above negativity; your experiences don't define you.

Some of the unpleasant sayings I heard about myself was the fact that I couldn't organise a reception for my husband's burial and I'm not able to put things in order in my hall. I may not be perfect at organising receptions or even putting things in order in my room, but I knew how to give a husband hope. I knew how to hold a husband's hand for him to stand up even at his lowest. I knew how to let a man walk with his head high when he was supposed to walk with his head bowed. I knew I was a godly wife, and a godly wife was enough.

In this life, know that people will try and convince you that they know you inside out when in truth, they don't. People will also project their fears on you, and others will look at you through their lenses that are either cracked or need a thorough cleaning.

Dear you, don't feel inadequate because you can't do one thing; feel adequate because of the 1000 things you can do. Always avail yourself for growth and learning. Know your worth and know that people who lose you are the losers, not you.

This Is Where We Are

A society that will focus on a widow's outlook and gestures to decide whether she loved her husband or not;

A society that chooses to apply tradition when it suits them;

A society that fails to think about the future of kids left behind but rather concentrate on what a widow does or does not do;

A society that will question why a widow steps out of her house to pick up her kids from school before the end of the 40 days and would sit her down to explain to her that a widow isn't supposed to go out before the 40 days so that at the end of the 40 days if there is a pregnancy, it would be easy to identify where it came from.

A society that is comfortable with taking an item that belongs to a deceased but telling a widow she can't have this or that.

At the end of the day, it is people who make up society. Choose to give life to people around you rather than stifle the air they breathe. It really starts with you!

Dear reader, it is a reality, but unfortunately, it becomes more obvious when you become a victim and not an onlooker. It becomes just a 'movie' or 'someone else's story' when you are not in it.

Just look around you and see the names given to widows. The heartbreaking part is that the majority of the backlash comes from fellow women.

Women will sit and analyse why a widow has a smile on her face while she's mourning;

Women will sit and analyse why a widow didn't cut her hair when her husband died;

Women will sit and analyse how a widow knows book but does not know the culture;

Women will sit and analyse why a widow chooses to wear black dresses and not Kaba and Slit.

Lessons

Dear widow/widower/ reader, these are personal lessons that widowhood life has taught me. It could serve as a rail on which to move your life out of misery and propel you to God's best for your life when life hands you lemons.

1. One thing that this journey has taught me is to have the confidence to tell God that "Let your will be done." I say it now, in a different way, with a different meaning, with sincerity, and without fear. At first, I used to say it, I believed that his way was perfect, but I said it, holding back a bit.

2. Another thing this journey has taught me is that when God decides to bless you, people around you will try to tell you that you do not deserve that blessing. They will ask oh, are you not the one who suffered? Are you not the one whose parents couldn't take care of you? Are you not the one who used to beg before you ate? Are you not the one…? Are you not the one...? They don't know that when God says it's time to shine, no one can argue about it. They don't know that God is God, and he decides whom to favour, whom to show mercy to, whom to bless, and whom to lift up. No one can change God's decrees because He is God alone.

3. This journey has also taught me that it is not okay to be in misery because people are too busy with their own

issues, and being in misery will not help you, and it will not bring you any good. You will remain in your misery forever. Don't be a burden to anyone. Be independent, grow up, pick yourself up and shine! Those who want you to remain in misery want their self-gratification. Always remember that the real work is done by you and only you. When it's time to get down and dirty, no one will get down with you. Please, no one by remaining in misery. Decide not to be a burden to people around you.

4. I've learnt to pay attention to myself so that I don't have to crave for attention from other people. I've learnt to be comfortable with myself, and I've learnt to be my own cheerleader in a world where there's too much noise and so much negativity.

5. I constantly remind myself that we are just passing through; this world is not our home. There's no point in playing God in another person's life; there will always be only one God. When you do good for others, don't let them feel indebted to you for the rest of their lives. Learn to free people and learn to free yourself, for life is short.

6. Most importantly, I have learnt that I must be still and know that He is God!

Grace

I have been asked several times what is making me survive this great tragedy of losing a husband in a bizarre manner. I keep saying it is the grace of God, and it is indeed the grace of God. It is by the grace of God that I am still alive and able to move around and take care of the kids. Some people decided to call the grace I am enjoying as disrespect to tradition, among others. But the grace of God is the grace of God, and I am enjoying it unapologetically.

I am an example of "every situation is a learning situation" because, over the years, I have learnt resilience from many situations that have come my way. I think I am the sum total of every little experience I have passed through. I have become stronger, better, and wiser. I will not change any of the experiences I have passed through. They have made me who I am.

Knowing Me

As a widow, you get to hear a lot more, especially when my case took the turn that it did. Sometimes, I wonder how well those who decided to make certain heart-wrenching comments knew me. I just want to save you, the reader, the stress of straining yourself to imagine who I am.

The God factor has always been there; let me take you back to when God changed our story and my dad got a decent job at Aluworks. One day, he entered a Redeemed Christian Church of God church at Mile 7 under the influence of alcohol. He decided to start attending church there, and he played the drums very well. A Sunday with my dad behind the drums was a joyful one. Since he became part of the church, we also became part of the church.

We went to a convention in Nigeria one day, and he dedicated himself to serving one of the elders in the church who was ill. The job at Aluworks came after that event because the man was one of the managers at the company. My father can serve! He doesn't care whether he is older than you or not; he will serve you. I remember there was a time when his weekend job was washing and ironing for a family who worked at the Electricity Company of Ghana. I believe serving is a gift from God. If you find yourself readily and happily wanting to serve others, see it as a gift, and don't let anyone make you feel less.

While at Aluworks, Christmas days were nice because the company always gave them canned drinks, rice, oil, chicken, corned beef, and all the nice things. Life was getting better for us, and childhood was becoming fun.

I remember my dad giving my siblings and me an offering for Sunday school and bread money because our Sunday school teachers at the time used to sell bread just in case the children got hungry. During offering time one Sunday, the teacher was surprised that my two brothers gave the same amount of offering, and I gave a higher amount. She had to ask why my money was higher, and I told her I decided to add my bread money to the offering money and she was shocked. Oh yes, at that age, I knew how to sow seeds.

I stood on our compound one day, looked up, and started singing, "When I look up the mountain, the valley, sea…" I had goosebumps as I pictured the greatness of God. I really felt that there was a great God somewhere. I kept singing the song over and over again. It really felt good. I felt God close. I was a child, not up to 10 years, but I knew the greatness of God, and I desired it.

We had hard times as a family. I could remember a day when it rained heavily and had rainwater in barrels. In my mind, the water was dirty because it came from the roof, so I wasn't comfortable drinking it. I looked into the big barrel, fetched the water with my cup, closed my eyes, and prayed to God to sanctify the water for me and take away every dirt from it. Not only did I feel my thirst quenched, but the water tasted like Fanta. I will never be able to explain that feeling to anyone properly because I felt, oh, they would say, its childish brain wanting to drink Fanta. There were times when as kids, all we had to eat was roasted corn gotten from people's farms because our parents had gone out to work, and somehow we had finished our lunch before lunch and were very hungry, and there was nothing to eat.

I am not shy to say that at about age 12, I was helping rich people in their homes with cooking, washing, and general home chores. I looked forward to the time I spent in their homes because I always liked the environment. It gave me something to look up to; it gave me a certain benchmark to aim at. I knew I wanted to be in such an environment, and I definitely knew that I would want my children to grow up in an environment where there was no lack. I was hard-working, and I loved to serve. I could look at the shoes my friends wore to school beautifully arranged on shelves, and

I imagined having the same one day and my children having the same. I never felt cheated and bitter; I only felt when it was time for me to have all the nice things I saw in rich people's homes, I would get them. It was nice listening to my rich friends telling their nannies to give them enough stew because they were growing.

Life became harder, and my dad's priorities changed; he wasn't coming home, and he wasn't bringing in salary for our fees. He used to bring food from work, and we looked forward to that. Even though sometimes he came as late as 10 pm or sometimes 11 pm, we always waited for the food. When he stopped coming home entirely, the food stopped, and we happened to be part of the children who were always called forward for owing school fees. It wasn't comfortable as we were sometimes sacked. We never used real school bags like other children but paper bags to store our books. Our silly rich friends could laugh and mock us to the core about them. You can imagine the times that we used torn paper bags. We attended a very good school, but things were falling apart because the center didn't hold.

My mother wove chair backs; we helped her with them and looked forward to people buying. We helped her make doughnuts which we sold in our class. She sold her African cloths to keep us going.

We finally had to leave the school we were in to find one we could afford the fees because my mother had to make the decision to enroll my elder sister in a nursery teacher training course. As young as I was, I looked after my big sister's child while she went to training.

My mother tirelessly used to creatively prepare dishes out of gari for us. However, one day, she ran out of ideas, and we got stuck with her simple version of gari foto, which was made from just gari and palm nut oil (red oil) with some spices. It was very nice, so we always requested for it, but my system had to reject it one day as I was tired of it. I vomited out gari foto one day at school. I never liked gari after that incident.

There was a time we were buying food on credit; my mother did barter trade with her big pans because she used to make Fante kenkey to sell, but health issues and the heat made her switch to weaving. From kenkey to banku to soup, just name it, we bought on credit. We bought foodstuff on credit, too, from yam to fish to sweet potatoes and any other thing we might need. We always faced the embarrassment of being stopped outside by creditors inquiring about the whereabouts of our mother. I have seen what poverty is, and I have seen what it means to have.

At some point, we stayed in a wooden structure that was not in good condition. We moved into uncompleted buildings but were in the same area with my maternal grandfather, who stayed in his house in Mile 7. At a point, we were even in a kiosk. We always had a positive attitude about life because my mother was always jovial as she had been a nursery teacher for years. She taught us nursery rhymes, and we used to sing and tell stories in the evenings.

She later switched to selling locally made powdered soap, and I was glad to come from school and go to the market at Dome railways with my pan on my head selling the powdered soap. One day, a friend's uncle saw me in the market and didn't like it, so when I came home, he sent for me to ask why I was selling, and I said I was doing it to help my mother. He didn't understand.

When we moved out from our school, my mum later went on a school hunt; she put my two brothers in a government school and went further to look for a private school for me to attend. Why she chose a private school for me, I still don't understand, but I am very grateful for that. My mum had wanted to grow up to become a doctor, but she was told she was a girl and school wasn't for her, and it was only witches who were clever in school. Her inability to further her education shattered her dreams, and I know she didn't want that path for me. In spite of her struggles, she made sure to put me in a private school. My elder brother didn't come to terms with leaving an international school to be in a government school.

We had to come back to my grandfather's house to have the luxury of being put in a proper room. Yes! We came back because we used to be with him. I cannot remember how old I was, but I know I was very little, about five years old, when he sacked my little brother and me from his house late in the night. I know he had many lands in that area but eventually sold all and kept the one he made home with his children and grandchildren in Mile 7, Accra.

My mother was not around because she was ill. My father had gone to work at a block factory, and my grandfather could not wait for my father to come home before sacking us. I held my little brother's hands, and I saw us walking up a hill towards nowhere in particular. I wonder where my father finally saw us, but he found us, and we made block factories, our homes, moving from one to the other. My resilience to situations started at such an early age!

Upon our return to the house, the only problem we encountered was the unnecessary quarrels that became unbearable because of so many relatives occupying various rooms in my grandfather's house. All his children and their children somehow found their way back into his house. He married a lot of wives, and as such, he had many children and grandchildren. Coupled with that, he later built small rooms on the big compound so he could rent out. I didn't like the environment at all because it was too chaotic for me. I started selling oranges in the evenings after school in front of my grandfather's house. I wasn't even 15 years yet when relatives started conditioning my mind to learning hairdressing after JHS because some tenants in my grandfather's house were hairdressers, and I helped them fix rollers. I felt it was wrong for them to think that after JHS, I would not be able to continue school, but I never said a word. I never allowed their limitation to change what I saw about myself. I saw myself going higher and higher. Children and young people must be encouraged to be the best they can be. If you are reading this today, know that generational limitation is real but thank God those who realise it and see the need to rise above it succeed with God's help.

As I mentioned early on, my mother fell ill. She always had tummy issues, and she was convinced she had an ulcer. She left for her aunt's house in the Eastern Region to stay with her for a while. Meanwhile, we were in our grandfather's house, fending for ourselves. We could have gone wayward, but somehow we were grounded. There were times we ate banku with just pepper that was plucked from our grandfather's compound with no tomatoes. We used to always make plenty of porridge that could take us throughout the day, even when my mother was around. You just have to know that if you feel hungry, there's porridge for you, and we were okay with it. Sometimes you had to know that all you had was lemon grass tea brewed. My mother taught us to be content with what we had, even if what we had was nothing. A little flashback to one day in the wooden structure. After cooking rice, we searched for money everywhere and couldn't get any, except a coin, so we had to go and buy sugar and just pour it on the rice and eat. Some children had come to the compound to play, and they could see through the room and realised we were eating cooked rice with sugar. They were disgusted and full of mockery, but we were not bothered. I always remembered the days when we had enough and the times we lacked. I started understanding the complexities of life and the impermanence of situations even as a child. I never missed my all-night prayer meetings because I really loved the atmosphere, and I always walked back home alone with reflections and serious conversations with God. I was never scared of darkness. I talked to God alone in the streets till I got home. A prophecy came one day that God would bring a lady my way to take care of me. I always wondered who the lady would be; I actually thought one of my rich friends' mothers would be the one. God started teaching me that his ways are not our ways, and he started teaching me that help will not come from where I expect it to come from. He started teaching me that I could not simply put him in a box.

My mother came back from the Eastern Region and had to be at the Achimota hospital for a very long time. She couldn't even pay hospital bills, so I stopped school to sleep in the hospital with her. I put a mat close to her bed and always slept by her because I wanted to take care of her. I ate the hospital food with her. I was in JHS 1, I think. The nurses could call me and say that my mother is about to die, so I should go back home and go to school and leave her in the hospital because her life is over, and mine is yet to begin. Maybe they felt they were giving a child candid advice, but that was unnecessary. That period of my life saw me walking alone through the Achimota forest into town to visit the people we knew could help with bills. Looking back, I realise I was fearless. I had a mission, and that was what occupied my mind; the mission to find help for my mother.

One day, I came from town, and my mum told me a lady came to pray with sick people at the hospital and paid her bills, and said she would come back to visit because she wanted to see this daughter who had left school to take care of her mother in the hospital. She did come back, and she engaged me in a conversation. She asked whether I wanted to continue school which I replied emphatically, "YES!" I can never stop going to school.

My mother was discharged whilst the lady sent me to my school, with fees paid in full. Although I had missed most of my classes, I was first in class for that term. My headmistress stayed in the school with her family, and based on request by one of her daughters, who was in my class and was a good friend, I joined them in the house until I wrote my last BECE paper. Thank you to the Acquaah-Arhin family for accommodating me. My dad came around to wish me well when I was writing my exams. He always stood by the bus that would take us to the center, waved, and said his best wishes. I don't know why, but I appreciated that a lot. This man always told me that I would be a great woman, and I held on to that saying. Although at a point in time, he was absent in our lives, his words and confidence in me always urged me on.

Dear fathers, speak life into the lives of your daughters. Dear parents, speak good things into the lives of your children because whatever you say will shape their lives.

Don't dampen their spirits. If you don't have good things to say, please keep quiet.

After my BECE, I moved in with my prophecy mum. Prior to moving in, I used to always go to her house after church to assist her with cooking and cleaning the house. The Bible says in Proverbs 18: 16, "A man's gift makes room for him and brings him before great men." By the grace of God, I have never been lazy. I saw a new kind of life, where you wake up and drink coffee, where you eat in posh restaurants and have sleepovers in nice hotels; where you attend big parties and learn how to hold wine glasses.

After Senior High School, I had so many hopes of going straight to the university. It was not to be, as I sat at home for one more year before going. I couldn't come to terms with not being in school. I felt alone. I felt hopeless. I was broken, felt empty, and couldn't see the direction of my life. At a point, I felt like dying. I felt like the ground should just open and swallow me. God was showing me that his time is the best and that he makes all things beautiful in his time. During this period of my life, daily broadcasts of Reverend Eastwood Anaba on Sunny FM dubbed "Wind of Change," which was later changed to "Wind of Love," gave me hope. One day, after the broadcast, I called the number, and the resident pastor's wife, Mrs. Rosemond Anchebah, picked up. I told her I felt lost, I didn't know the direction my life was taking, and I needed to speak with someone. She invited me to one of the upcoming programmes that Reverend Eastwood organises - Possessing the Land Rally. I went for the programme and had a de-stressing chat with Mrs. Anchebah after.

During that time also, I decided to visit a Lighthouse Chapel opposite our house in Dome. The first day I stepped foot there, I felt at home and welcomed. I said to myself that I would want to stay. The resident bishop's wife hugged me when the first-timers were asked to stand. God knew I needed that hug because I had cried that morning in the house before going to the service. That hug, I think God himself came down to give it because I haven't been able to explain how I felt. I understood that day that a pastor's wife is supposed to be so in tune with God that she can be able to show the right gestures at the right time and relate well with the members such that invisible burdens are lifted.

When I finally got admission into the university, the next obvious challenge to tackle was how to pay my school fees. I was, however, disappointed as the avenue I anticipated on getting the funds from couldn't materialise. I felt so disappointed, empty again, sad, and confused. At the time my fees needed to be paid, my prophecy mum was struck with cancer, and money had to be channeled into her treatment abroad. It was time to take care of herself. I cried every evening. I felt life was against me. Neither my dad nor anyone around me had the means to pay for my fees. God used that experience to improve my sensitivity to his voice. If only we would be still and know that He is God, He will speak to us. My tears during that period would have made a dam overflow. I simply had no one; I felt lost. One night after reading Joseph's story in my Bible and how God remembered him in prison, I prayed and told God to remember me. After praying, it just occurred to me to call a certain blessed and favoured woman, and I did, and the following day, my school fees was paid. God has miraculously positioned people, especially women, to make an impact in my life. To offer help when I need it. I do not take it for granted. We have good women in society, and I aim to be one myself, holding the torch for younger women.

I say to God's glory that prophecy mum remains cancer free to date and I appreciate her sensitivity to God and for availing herself for God to use her to change my life. You have a special place in my heart MUM!

I understand what it means for God to say His plans are not our plans. If we could take a stand to fully trust God and his timings, we would not hold grudges; we would not harbour bitterness against people. Understand the roles of people in your life and understand that times and seasons are real. God has everything planned. The puzzles will fit in perfectly. Also, understand that people will come for a season, and when their seasons are over in your life, don't become bitter. Open up yourself for God to do what He wants to do.

Dear reader, your struggles in life shouldn't be a limitation but rather a motivation to be a highflyer. Dream big. Challenge yourself. Make a name for yourself. Always remember you deserve nothing but the best.

Reality Of The Loss

I've found myself in the widowed category; therefore, I cannot stop myself from thinking deeply about the word 'Widow'. In the beginning, I didn't like the sound of the word widow being associated with me. I always said silently in my head that I am not a widow. Maybe I was living in a state of self-denial. I actually told myself that my husband had just traveled, hoping to reunite with him one day. Now, I have come to accept the title, but in a positive way.

After serious pondering, I came to the conclusion that one can still be married and have the widow mentality. The widow mentality, to me, is total surrendering to God, looking up to only God, focusing on Him, and knowing that He is your only provider. He will direct men to come to your aid; He will choose your helpers for you. You will not rely on your own strength, you will not rely on your beauty, and you will not rely on your certificates. Just Him!

I have taken a keen interest in widows in the Bible and what God made out of their lives, their roles, and the impacts they had. Dare to make an impact in every situation you find yourself in. You are where you are for a purpose. Your pain will make sense. Your pain will not be wasted.

The widow who gave two coins: She teaches me that you can have nothing but still give out your best. That widow had no money, but she had love and faith that pushed her to give all the money she had on her to God. She emptied herself. God cannot give us things when our hands are full. You need to pour out yourself; you need to empty yourself in order to receive. Dear widow, pour your grief on God. Exchange it for a lightness of heart and happiness. This widow who gave her two coins was recognized due to the genuineness and purity of her heart. The Bible admonishes us to guard our hearts because everything else flows from them. This widow could have chosen to complain because she had every reason to. Was she not a poor widow? Wasn't she left with only her last two coins? She could have held on to her last coins. Learn to let go when you are supposed to.

I am very sure people around her thought she was a fool for what she did. Christians of today grumble about everything, including someone's generosity. Someone called me to say that I shouldn't give all my money to the church. You would be surprised that while you are busy grieving, words that you never imagined could be said to you would be said. Keep your heart pure. People would not understand your walk with God, which is expected but just remember that God does not make fools out of the people who love Him right. You are the only one who will understand the kind of faith you have in God and how it benefits you. God doesn't put those who trust in Him fully to shame. He is a rewarder.

The widow of Zarephath: Why would God choose a widow whose resources were drying up and who had the sole intention of awaiting death with her son after everything got finished? Her story teaches me obedience even in the storm. You can still hearken to God's voice, and you can trust him even when all you have is nothing. God preserved the widow and her child, as well as Elijah. It teaches me that the purpose we are called to should never die with the storm. You can survive the storm and preserve your purpose to glorify God's name only when you obey. Check those you listen to when you are in the storm because that will determine your survival or otherwise. Sometimes the still, small voice in your head whispering peace and calm to you is the voice of God guiding you. Because of the still, small voice, you may act differently and appear to the crowd as weird, stupid, useless, and foolish. People around you will be blamed for giving you wrong advice when they haven't even given you any advice. When you are on the right path with your actions, you have peace and calm from within. Grant us a spirit of discernment, oh God!

The widow and the unjust judge: This is a persistent widow who never stopped asking. This story teaches me not to be quiet when my voice can bring a change in a situation. Find your voice, stand up for yourself, and stand up for your rights. I haven't stopped asking God to keep fighting for my children and me. If the unjust judge gave in to the widow's demands, God will listen to the pleas of his children. The storms will come but may they not carry you away, and may you not be drowned. In order to survive the storm, you have to keep connected to the source - God. Be persistent, keep asking, keep knocking, keep seeking, and do not leave God.

Naomi, Ruth, and Orpah: These three powerful women had a purpose; they were smart, they were wise, and they were full of love. From my own interpretation, life had dealt with them in the cruelest way, but Naomi was still filled with love and goodwill towards Ruth and Orpah. Naomi never looked down on Ruth and Orpah's pain. She never downgraded their pain. She was a widow who had lost two of her sons, but her love account was still full. She never told them that she was suffering more than them. Naomi teaches me that you can still be in pain; you can lose everything and still not be hateful and resentful. Naomi could have been manipulative, but she wasn't. Didn't she fear being alone?

Without a husband, without her sons? For her to tell Orpah and Ruth to go away, Naomi was a strong woman.

Orpah teaches us that sometimes, it's okay to say goodbye and find your own path. Her message to me is simple. Goodbyes are painful, but sometimes, one needs to let go. Her destiny obviously wasn't tied with Naomi and Ruth. People may say she was indecisive and easy to convince, but the question is, what was God's purpose for her? To me, she knew what she wanted, and she went for it. She wanted to go back, and she did. Her season in that land was over.

Ruth's steps were ordered by God. God had predestined that Naomi would guide her into her destiny, and it was so because of her obedience and her ability to follow. The people you follow and receive advice from can determine whether you will miss opportunities or not. When in grief, may progressive people surround you and remind you of the task ahead. May you not be burdened with traditions and ways that please men. You matter. Your progress matters. Your sanity matters. Your life matters. Your destiny matters. Your calling matters.

Abigail: Nabal's wife, who was both wise and beautiful, got married to David. She had a good heart and was wise. She saw the mistake Nabal made by not giving David and his men a portion of his meat and corrected it. Her good qualities drew her to David after her husband passed away. Abigail had a kind heart. She played an important role in David's life, and God didn't forget. She teaches me that, with a good heart, one can turn a bad situation around. With a good heart, you can preserve the lives of the people around you. She never judged; she just loved and showed kindness.

These women in the Bible show us that our suffering will not be in vain. There is hope for those who diligently seek the Lord.

Christians are not called to only enjoy, but the call of suffering is part of the package in following Christ. No matter the religion you belong to, you cannot run away from suffering because we live in a wicked world. When Jesus said in Matthew 16: 24, "Whoever wants to be my disciple must deny themselves and take up their cross and follow me," He didn't mince words at all.

I decided to take up my cross of suffering, of being a widow, and fight for myself and my children. I found myself whispering one day that I am going to wear my suffering badge with grace. I don't know what that means, but I believe that God has given us the strength to shine when life's storms hit us so hard. Expect storms in this life and make up your mind to come out victorious. SHINE! When you approach problems with a defeatist mentality, you do not get anywhere. Be positive. Speak life and hope.

One rude awakening any widow should come to terms with is a failure of well-wishers to live up to the "we will take care of your kids" talk. All you might get is a push and assistance, but you have to know that your children are your responsibility, and you are your own responsibility. It is safer and better to have at the back of your mind that 99.9% of the responsibility lies on you.

Also, take note that people will overlook your daily struggles but become offended when they see your happy moments. When you wake up at dawn to cry, no one is there, so why should you bother about people getting headaches for your happy moments?

Independence

Life after the burial of Maxwell began when I became independent by moving out of Burma Camp. People in the camp thought it was weird for me to step out of a 'haven'; the no utility bills environment. But the truth was that I would have to leave someday and face the realities of life.

I had to now battle with being a father and a mother to my children. I had to battle the daily issues of life alone, especially when it had to do with the children. There are many instances where I felt overwhelmed. I have shared a few of such situations below:

Scenario 1: Jaden fell ill one day, and I sent him to the hospital. I cried the whole time. He was admitted, and they had to put drips on him. Anytime he started to cry, I cried too, and I think the nurse cried, too, at some point. These situations are overwhelming because they make it seem as if you will never be enough because your support system is no more. Take a deep breath; God's got you.

Scenario 2: Jerry was ill on a different occasion, and on our way from the hospital, I broke into tears. He wasn't sure what was happening, so he tapped me, I turned back, and he saw tears in my eyes, and he also started crying. Then I told him, "It's okay, I'm sorry, we'll be fine." He nodded and sat at the back quietly. This scenario, I can't explain it well. It was a deep feeling; we had unspoken words as our eyes were dulled with unanswered questions. I was thinking about how Maxwell being around would have helped the situation. There was a day Jaden hit his mouth on our center table and shifted a tooth; Maxwell told me to go ahead to work and that he would take him to the hospital and update me later. On this day, Maxwell was not around to see his Jerry with sores in his mouth so painful that, for days, he couldn't eat. This scenario made me sad because the reality that these kids would not have their father around them dawned on me.

Scenario 3: Same night. Jerry couldn't sleep. He was in pain, crying, so I couldn't sleep too. I played "Healing rain is falling down" by Michael Smith as I prayed, and I cried more than Jerry, who was in pain. He stopped crying, looked at me, and the look on his face was that of disapproval. But I was glad he saw me up warring at dawn, showing him that there's a part of life where you have to deny yourself of sleep and claim what is yours through prayer. He heard me cry and say, "God, please heal Jerry." Maxwell and I would have stayed up in the night praying for Jerry to get well.

Scenario 4: On our way to school conversations…

Jerry: Mummy, our daddy is with Jesus?

Me: Yes.

Jaden: Mummy, what did you say?

Me: Daddy is with Jesus.

Jerry: What is Jesus telling our daddy?

Me: (wanting to get lost from the car, I didn't expect this) He's telling your daddy that we are fine. You enjoy swimming, and currently, we are heading to school.

Jerry: (pleased with the answer) smiles.

Jaden: So what is our daddy telling Jesus?

Me: He's telling Jesus to keep looking after us.

A different day

Jaden: So mummy, now that our daddy is in heaven, who will be our daddy now?

Me: (Quietness) No one.

Jaden: Jesus?

Me: Yes, Jesus. But Jaden, sometimes a child has only a mother to take care of him, and it's very okay. Other times, a child's father and mother are all in heaven, and they have other family members to take care of them. So appreciate the fact that you have a mother to take care of you, okay?

Jaden: Okay (not convinced).

Another day

Jaden: Mummy, buy me a dog.

Me: Okay, Jaden, we can't have a dog where we are now, so wait a bit.

Jaden: Jerry, do you remember when we were in the other house, and our daddy was around? We had a white dog. Daddy told us he was travelling and never came back.

Jerry: Yes. Mummy, has our daddy died?

Silence...

Deep questions

Jerry: Mummy, does our daddy still have his gun?

Me: No.

Jaden: Why?

Me: Because he doesn't need a gun in heaven.

Jerry: Why doesn't he need a gun?

Me: Because there are no bad people in heaven

Pause...

Jaden: Mummy, what is our daddy's number?

Me: He doesn't have a number.

Jaden: Why?

Me: Because he doesn't need a number in heaven.

Jerry: Did he leave his phone in that house?

Me: Yes.

Some minutes later

Jerry: Mummy, where is our daddy's pickup?

Me: It is not around.

Jerry: Oh, then our daddy will walk.

I have to battle all these questions from my boys, tackle numerous issues of life, and still keep my sanity. It indeed overwhelms me sometimes.

Dear widow, whatever it is, do not lose your focus! Decide what is important and what isn't. Just do not lose focus while you are grieving.

I painstakingly chronicled events after the burial of my late husband, which I wish to share with you, dear reader, so you can appreciate the struggles widows sometimes go through alone when everyone leaves after the funeral.

Days like These

18th June 2017: Father's Day: I was up throughout the night. I made a WordPress post at dawn wishing Maxwell a Happy Father's Day in heaven. Reverend Eastwood Anaba sent me a beautiful and thoughtful message about how I now have to play the fatherly role as well as my motherly role. He wished me a Happy Father's Day. I cried after I read the message.

27th June: I drove the kids to school myself, and I fought back the tears. First time driving after 29th May 2017. I drove them and picked them, and it remained so; we became used to the routine. Daddy was no more to pick them up in the afternoons. The first reality hit me. Will you remain broken and helpless when your kids need you? I think I was always ahead of myself in my thoughts, preparing for possible scenarios and situations that may arise after the ceremonies.

June was quite difficult because after the funeral, in my quiet moments, I would pull Maxwell's burnt pictures and cry myself to sleep. I wanted to let everything sink in without anyone's help. I started getting heart pains. This episode continued till early August. How wicked and inhumane and barbaric can human beings who were created in God's image be! The heart of man is indeed desperately wicked. Selfishness abounds, and someone's selfishness has caused my family great pain. It has changed our lives forever.

One sad thing is that we never know when we will die, and because death is impromptu, we may not always be able to settle some issues and clear the air on some things.

Dear widow, grieving and trying to clear the air on some issues is too much work. When you realise you will always be misunderstood, and nothing you do will be appreciated by some people, relax and live. You know your heart, and God knows your heart, and it is enough. Choose the issues that will give you stress, and when you have children, you know that enough stress will come from them. Stick to your priorities. Don't expect everyone to like you, believe in you, cheer you on, and defend you. The people God chooses to root for you will do so effortlessly without expecting you to suffocate for them.

July 2017: This month was full of hearing ridiculous things. I heard that I am a wicked and heartless woman, the only reason for being able to read my tribute in the manner I did. Another questioned posed was that do I think I'm the only one who had gone to school and hence could read my tribute without even making a mistake or pausing? The popular audio that circulated was a backlash on the sunglasses I wore during the funeral. It was said that I wore cheap sunglasses at the burial and didn't cry whilst the whole of Ghana was crying for me. Isn't it funny that at a time like this, someone would be concerned about sunglasses and how cheap they were? Someone also said she entered my room and saw me watching the video of Maxwell being killed, and I was laughing and eating. In July, I understood that when people want to see you miserable, and you fail to be, they try all means to make you miserable, and mostly, the mouth will be the tool. In July, I understood that it's difficult for some people to just keep quiet when they have nothing to say.

In July, the Akosombo and Accra Tennis clubs organised a tournament to honor Maxwell. I got to the tennis court and started crying because Maxwell and I had been there a few times, and now I was there with the kids; a group of guys were playing, and he wasn't part. Life is a bit funny because things were happening that had happened before but this time, under different circumstances.

I look back and realise that the reality of losing a loved one is shocking, and the ability to contain the shock goes a long way to help in managing the effects of the loss.

August 2017: I started attending all-night services. I just wanted to be in tune with God. I didn't want to feel that I was withdrawing from God. I was lost for words at my first all-night church service; I didn't know what to say to God. I was so used to praying for Maxwell that now it felt odd to be standing there and not praying for him. I was quiet for a long time; then I started praying for Jaden and Jerry; for their well-being and many other issues.

In August, I enrolled in an online course on impulse. I wanted to do something different and to stretch myself beyond limits. It was exciting for me, and I liked the fact that something would keep my mind occupied. I didn't want to spend time feeling pity for myself. It was exciting for me because Maxwell and I had always talked about the fact that we may end up always studying one course or the other. He used to tell the kids that their parents are forever students and they won't have any option but to love studying too. Anytime we sat by the table in our room to discuss educational topics and sometimes share what to research on, it was a great feeling. There's nothing like a husband and wife who understand each other's dreams and are dedicated to making sure that the dreams are realised because they understand that they are all working towards one goal and one future. They understand that divided they fall, together they stand.

On our anniversary, I went away with the kids to a quiet place. My pastors visited, as well as close friends. They brought flowers, cakes, drinks, and biscuits for the kids. I cried throughout the day. I am grateful for the wonderful people around me. In the evening, my girls dragged me out of bed to go watch a movie with the kids at the mall. I was happy they did because we laughed throughout.

September 2017: My 30th Birthday fell in this month. First birthday in seven years without Maxwell. I received ten cakes from friends and family. I made sure to update my status with every cake. I, later on, heard that people were offended by the fact that I was counting my cakes, and I dared to enjoy the day a little. They wondered what more I wanted from my dead husband by writing on my status that the cakes were flowing and Maxwell should let more flow. They concluded on the fact that I'm so materialistic that I'm asking a dead husband to let cakes flow. What they didn't know was that at the back of my mind, I kept reminding myself of how I was a widow at age 30 and how I felt it was unfortunate to be married at 25 and be a widow at 30. When you are born, there's no note attached to your forehead to let you know of the life-changing experiences that will hit you. Leave people to decide how they want to go through their life experiences.

People would do anything to see you down and further down because, in their minds, other people do not deserve to be up; they do not deserve to be happy. Take note that your happiness is not in anybody's pocket. Take charge of your happiness, and remember, God wants you happy.

A friend from London fixed a spa date for me, and I totally enjoyed it. The massage helped me to understand that I had been tensed for too long, and my muscles were not relaxing. I had frequent headaches. I made a decision to have regular massages instead of falling on Valium. Anytime I entered the spa subsequently, the lady would ask me whether my headaches had improved. It was a wake-up call to me to really pay attention to my emotions and control how negative things affected me.

October 2017: Full-time work started. I decided to drop the kids at school in the mornings and let someone pick them up in the afternoons. Anytime I dropped them and headed towards the route that led to my workplace, my eyes were full of tears. One day, my tears actually blinded me before I became aware of the fact that I could end up in an accident one of the days if I kept on with that all the time.

I missed Maxwell because he would have been there. Our normal morning routine involved him washing my car in the morning after he came from personal training while I prepared breakfast. He sometimes offered to drop the kids off for me when I was running late, and he always picked them up from school when they closed, except he was away. That afternoon bonding time wouldn't be there anymore, and the fun the kids had in the afternoons would be scrapped. No more yoghurt time, no more pool time, no more tennis time. It was painful. I felt sad for them.

The drive home after work has always been a lonely one, sometimes full of tears. Sometimes I picture how life is like in heaven and what Maxwell could be doing. Sometimes I talk to God, asking him how Maxwell is, and then I pinch myself and say, Really, am I really asking God that?

November 2017: Maxwell's birthday was in this month. First birthday in heaven. I did the usual breakfast and gave it out to a needy woman and her kids by the roadside. I felt fulfilled. I tried not to cry that day. I went to work as usual, and after work, I passed through GhOne Television to give a little speech on what Mob Justice means to me. That also got some level of disapproval from some people who felt I talked about my husband too much and asked if I was the only one who had lost a husband. Some people also felt I was enjoying the popularity that I had gained through Maxwell's death. People will always be people.

Seven months later, someone picked on me and said, "The poor Barbara is now calling someone needy." I referred to the woman by the roadside as needy, and that was an issue.

I slept and woke up in a room with my kids; I got to the roadside, and a pavement was home to someone, can't I call her needy? If I have two dresses and someone is naked, can't I call the person needy? If I have peace and joy, and someone doesn't, the person needs peace and joy, and that person can be called needy. We all have needs, including the very wealthy people we know. If you find yourself paying attention to a person's actions and inactions only to pass judgements, it's time to wake up, you are sliding into dangerous grounds, and you may not be able to come out of it. We are too critical of others.

In this month, I understood the depth of selfishness in human beings. Someone sent a message to another person pretending to be me and actually sent it through my number without having access to my phone. I kept asking myself why the person would be so heartless to do such a thing at such a time.

I needed a new space and a new environment and November was the month to do that, so I did. I felt the responsibility of looking for a place I liked, the responsibility of deciding what curtains to use, what bed to use, and deciding how I wanted the space to look, to make the kids and I have a serene atmosphere. I loved the experience of owning my decision. One of Maxwell's friends from AIS and one of my many unknown people who became like sisters after the incident were involved from start to finish, and the help was a relief.

On Christmas day, my bishop's wife, Reverend Adelaide Heward-Mills, sent us a beautiful package that included bags of rice, drinks, meat, etc., enough to last us for many months. Her Christmas giftings were repeated every year after that. I must say the body of Christ has given us unflinching support.

December 2017: A solemn month as I pondered about life and the fact that I started the year with Maxwell but will be ending without him. I had a painful experience where someone gave me an attitude in the presence of her husband. It felt like she knew she had the support of her husband. It went deeper than it should have, so I cried a little. In December, I realised that it is important for us to not allow our pain to eat us up so much so that when we see a picture of what could have been us, we become pained. We need to constantly remind ourselves that our pain doesn't define us, but God defines us, and we are what He says we are, not what we've been through.

31st December night: I wrote, "Lying in bed, crying, thinking about how last year's 31st December night was spent with Maxwell, but I am alone this year and would go to church alone; he's not with us, and it's painful".

If only we could have a glimpse of tomorrow, we would be a little more loving, a little more caring, a little kinder, a little more agreeing, understanding, and forgiving. It's never too late; make sure you cherish each moment and that you hold your loved ones close!

January 2018: Usually, after the 31st Night Service, we come home and have a drink and toast to the New Year. I didn't get to do that this year, and it felt weird and, frankly, lonely with a lot of flashbacks.

10th January: I cried till I slept because I listened to Blakk Rasta's song he made for Maxwell. To be honest, there were too many pictures in my mind and too many what-ifs. A lot of questions that would never be answered. The mind feels pressured sometimes.

12th January: I wrote, "Dear Diary, when your son wakes up at dawn to ask of his daddy, you ask yourself, "Where is the crowd that tried to dictate to you how you should mourn your husband?" People are quick to provide solutions they feel are best for your problems; they provide one size fit all answers, but life isn't like that, and if we can learn to accommodate the feelings, passion, and differences of people around us, most of our problems would be solved.

12th January evening: "Dear Diary, today is the first time I stepped into smoothies after Maxwell's passing. I just stared at where we sat the last time we were there with the kids. I remember clearly we were taking pictures, and the kids were playing. Dear diary, I can't go anywhere without memories; the journey is a rollercoaster one. I was undecided about the smoothie combination I should buy because Maxwell always chose, so I settled on number 16. I think I got it wrong; it didn't taste like what Maxwell used to order!

13th January: "Dear Diary, I decided to massage Jerry's feet today, the way I used to do it for Maxwell, and it was fun". Little things count. Cherish every moment. You may be left with only memories when a loved one passes away, and it would be sad if the memories you created together were bitter memories or if the last encounter was bitter.

17th January: "Dear Diary, now I'm not sure about the songs 'Onise Iyanu' by Nathaniel Bassey and 'Still you Reign' by Sonnie and Annie Badu. I think I over-listened to the songs when the news of Maxwell's passing was broken to me. Now I listen, tear up and play the whole scene of the delegation breaking the news to me in my mind again and again. These songs remind me so much of the most painful moments in my life, but I appreciate the fact that they kept me going. I started to remember when the delegation walked in on Monday night to tell me of the accident and when they walked in on Tuesday morning to tell me he had passed away. I'm sure I looked too broken and lost and fragile in their eyes. They couldn't stay for long; they couldn't look at me. But I had my playlist, and I had my God by my side. The words of Nathaniel Bassey, "I've tasted of your power, you have shown me so much mercy, my eyes have seen, my ears have heard..." gave me some assurance and hope. I kept reminding myself that I could not start blaming God because, truthfully, I've tasted his mercies and his goodness before. Sonnie Badu's words, "Still you reign, still you are king; still, you rule," kept ringing in my ears because God won't stop being God. His reign will not end, and his kingship will not end because I've been hit in the cruelest way I could ever imagine. This is not the time to be bitter; this is the time to show him that I believe in his power; I believe in his unchanging nature. I believe that he is good and will forever remain good.

I made a note in my diary that I miss doing little things: Serving food, removing boots and socks, making orange juice, making lemon tea, etc. Cherish the everyday happenings and the little memories you can gather from each day.

I made another note that said: Now when I hear Diaso; my heart skips a beat. When I hear "galamsey", everything keeps coming back to me.

18th January: "Dear Diary, feeling down since last night. I woke up the same, been crying my eyes out, and telling God to heal me because it still hurts. I will wipe my tears and step out to work because I need to be there for the kids."

Sometimes you are your only encouragement because most people around you are looking at you with some critical eyes. It's like they are waiting for you to fail so they can rejoice. If you want to wait for encouragement from such people, you will end up more depressed because the little things you even do to keep yourself happy offend them.

19th January: "How is it that you are not going to come back?" So unbelievable, like a dream, like a puzzle. Why does life have to be so mysterious? Then I asked myself whether the mysterious nature is in life or in growing up. Children easily bounce back, they easily forgive, and they don't hold grudges. Why did Jesus say that unless we become like little children, we cannot enter into God's kingdom? Maybe the solution to taking it easy in life and not ending up with too many scars is to be like a child; carefree, forgiving, not either trying to have the solution for every problem or to be all-knowing. Be happy, cry, laugh, jump, learn, fall, rise up, fall again and rise up, just love and be guided by life's manual– God's Word.

February 2018: On Valentine's Day, I went through the day with nothing special in mind. However, my colleagues had booked dinner for us at the Labadi Beach Hotel to celebrate the day. So I called a driver to meet us with the kids. Jerry kept mentioning daddy; as usual, Jaden was not in the mood to socialise, so he played games, and they refused to eat because they were already full. Everything fell apart, tumbling down in my mind because I missed my husband. I fought back tears until I could no longer hold them back. I started crying in front of my colleagues, making them feel bad. They consoled me and later started cracking jokes. I felt a bit sad. Ed Sheeran's song "Thinking out Loud" was playing; Maxwell and I used to hum that song together. I saw couples dancing; it was hard for me.

Our usual Valentine's Day tradition I came up with was to spend the night at home and make an elaborate dinner, so we just enjoy our company without being in an open space with other people. I cooked every day, but I did special cooking on birthdays, Valentine's Day, and Maxwell's friends coming over kind of days. I miss all these activities.

Again, I say cherish moments and build beautiful memories with your loved ones.

March 2018: 5th March was the first hearing of the court case in a high court. I knew I wouldn't be there, but I knew it would be a difficult day, and the rest of the court hearings would be difficult. I cried myself to sleep on the 4th and still woke up on the 5th crying. I didn't even know why I was crying, but I knew my husband was no more, and those who took his life were standing trial. It hurt to think that things turned out that way. Why did he have to go in such a manner?

17th March was Jaden's first birthday after the death of Maxwell. One thing led to the other, and he got a nice little party with a total of twelve cakes. I tried not to cry that day, but I kept thinking about how Jaden would not cut his cakes with his dad again. He would have been a great life coach for the boys; he was so full of wisdom. What a loss! I couldn't help but remember that the day Maxwell was leaving for the village, he called Jaden and told him that he was now the man of the house and that he should take good care of the home as well as me and Jerry. He told Jaden he would be back, but he never came back.

21st March was another court day, and the accused persons pleaded not guilty. I just said to myself, "WOW! I couldn't believe my ears. It sounded ridiculous, but they said that is the law, and we just have to bear the back and forth of the examinations and cross-examinations till they are proven guilty.

28th March was open day in the boys' school: I passed by the school before going to work; I looked through their books for the term, and I felt a knot in my throat. I would have gone with Maxwell, or he would have gone alone so I wouldn't be late for work. "Jaden drew us in a funny way, Maxwell. I still don't know which one is me and which one is you". I had mixed feelings on my way back to work, and the day was never the same.

In the evening, I wrote, "Maxwell, after work on my way home, I missed you, and it happens a lot because it's like I'm going home knowing you are not around to ask me how my day went. I played back the day you were very ill after an exercise in the bush. I remembered your head on my lap on the bed as I prayed for you silently with tears in my eyes so you wouldn't see me crying. I ended up crying in the car, remembering how you told me to bear with you because you had no appetite for food, making you refuse to eat anything I made. We were not even married by then. Today, you are no more, and people are questioning if I ever loved you because, in their opinion, I didn't cry when the whole of Ghana was crying with me."

April 2018: On 6th April, I just decided to stop being lazy and start documenting my journey, keeping in mind the one-year anniversary coming soon. I just knew Maxwell would frown upon the fact that I have sat down a whole year without coming out with something solid. I decided I had to write the book!

On 11th April, I passed the graveside with a colleague after work; I stood there and looked at the heap of sand. She said I should say something then I asked why? I had tears in my eyes. I told her you are not in the ground, you are up there, a spirit, but she insisted, and I said hi to you in my head and added, "You know you have a special place in my heart."

Driving back home, I told myself that great people don't stay down when they fall; they rise! I got home, wrapped myself to sleep, felt sad and moody; I couldn't sleep well, so I woke up at 3 am to start planning and decided to just go for a shop I had postponed going for because I felt it was expensive. A shop for sewing. We had planned the clothing line together, and I kept remembering that the day Maxwell passed away, I sent the final logo for his approval, but it was too late.

Stop postponing plans and ideas; just do it. Accomplish something. Just try. You can fail; it's fine, don't say you won't try because you are scared of failure.

12th April: There was a hearing, and as usual, I expected to see the update in the media, so when I saw the headline "Major Mahama's killers reject jury", my heart kept beating till I started getting headaches. I asked myself when will this end. An achievement for the day was that I paid for the shop.

13th April: Feeling dull and demotivated, the roller coaster journey is like that. I started imagining how the shop would look when it was done, what colour of paint to use, and where to put what. Then the logo came to mind again, and I decided I had to add the Maxwell element to it, and I became excited and energised. I asked myself what the Maxwell element would be. I love the adinkra symbols, and I settled on the adinkrahene, which symbolises greatness, charisma, and leadership, and my heart melted; that's the Maxwell element because he was great, he was a leader, and he had charisma, and I shouted in my head "YES! LET'S DO THIS".

When you feel down, just change your thoughts and experiment with ideas. Maybe a major innovative idea that will change the world may come from that moment.

16th April: Case was adjourned again, jury problems. I just said to myself thank God the boys are young and don't have to know all these updates. Around 9 pm, Jerry asked me whether I was tired, and I said yes. Then he asked whether I would cry, so I asked him why, and he said he saw me crying at 3 am when he was asleep. I just rolled my eyes. Children of today!

20th April: At dawn, I just woke up to think, and I told myself that it's still unbelievable that Maxwell is no more. The saying that two heads are better than one is really true. The loneliness and the stress from making decisions alone are just draining. It's not that I can't make decisions on my own, but life is much easier when you get along so well with someone, and it's as if your thoughts are always in sync, and someway somehow, he's able to tell you things you need to hear and things you need to do. It's like your second self, your reality!

May 2018: 1st May was full of memories because, on 1st May 2017, we were out and about. We visited one of Maxwell's aunties, and we did a short video. I kept playing the video over and over again, looking at Maxwell so full of life and asking myself how it was possible that he was no more. Videos and pictures are good memories, in my opinion. I later heard that people were asking why I was still posting about Maxwell, and the famous question, "is she the only one who has lost a husband" was asked.

Seriously, that question confuses me because I don't understand why someone would ask such a question. I can't stop people from posting about their dead husbands, and how anyone wants to remember their dead relatives is a personal choice. Don't we see people talking about their dead brothers and sisters many years after they pass on?

4th May was Jerry's 3rd birthday, and I felt happy making his birthday breakfast; I felt light and happy. I made it to work knowing Jerry would be cutting one of his many cakes in school. I came home late from a programme at work. I undressed and started crying. I cried my eyes out till my head started aching. I asked myself why I was crying, and I couldn't pinpoint what exactly was making me cry. I felt lonely. I told God that I might be crying because it feels good to be helpless in front of him. I slept feeling tired from all the crying.

5th May: We went to our usual morning prayers. I went to sit down and had to come out into the car to cry a bit. The previous night's crying was still not enough for the body. I came back into the church after wiping my tears and looked at the puffiness under my eyes.

After the service, we prepared to go to a playground in East Legon called Colabo, a nice place!

9th May: I made a note- "Just feeling dull, work closed, and I had no motivation. Maybe it's because the next court hearing is tomorrow, and I'm dreading reading the entire outcome on the internet." I passed through Unique Floral to order for wreaths for the anniversary. Driving back home, I kept sighing. I got home and wrote that I think the reason why I've been a bit down is because everything is dawning on me. The one year is fast approaching. Seriously, I don't know what phase of the grieving process I am in, but all I imagine is Maxwell running away and the people pursuing him. Being truthful to yourself helps in the grieving process. This is the stage I am in now; Jesus take the wheel. I never watched the video, I heard he pleaded for his life, but the wicked people only heard the voices in their heads urging them to carry on with their wicked and inhumane intention. Never pausing for a minute to assess the situation.

10th May: I had fun with the kids in the car before dropping them at school. I kept telling myself that every day must be a fun day because it was mostly so with their dad.

At work: "I'm a bit restless because I know the court hearing is in progress, and my heart is beating. I just want to know the next step and the outcome of the hearing. The news from Myjoyonline flashed in my face". Report: "State leads first witness as Major Mahama case begins" my heart skipped. I clicked to read; tears flowed as I read, "He was attacked, stripped, stoned, and killed by marauding residents of Denkyira Obuasi who claimed to have mistaken him for an armed robber..." "A different nurse then told me an armed robber who had been shot was at the mortuary. When we got there, I was shocked to see that person who was dead was Captain Mahama, who was lying naked".

I hoped my colleague didn't notice me crying; it's painful. I looked at Maxwell's picture and closed the story to continue with my work, but the tears kept flowing. Maxwell's aunty Martha called, and I couldn't pretend I was not crying. She told me to stop crying and put on makeup. The tears wouldn't stop, so I put my earpiece in my ears and played "Glory to the lamb", a song a pastor friend suggested I should always listen to when I'm down. By the time that song finished playing, the tears were gone, and then I listened to "You deserve the Glory", which automatically brightened up my mood because it urged me to think about how great God is. I whispered, "Thank You," and continued my work. I went back to check the stories, and for the very first time, I looked at the picture of the people standing trial, and I said to myself, are they that young? Or I'm confused.

Almost 6 pm

I wrote: "Sitting at my desk very frustrated because the taxi driver that picks up the boys hasn't sent them home at 5:50 pm and he won't pick his calls, and the teachers have confirmed he picked them up. It's not easy, ooo".

13th May: Mother's day- I spent the day going through our previous chats and saw last year's mother's day chats. After church, I picked up some flowers I had bought to be planted at the cemetery.

14th May: I passed by the cemetery in the morning before work and handed over the flowers to the workers. Standing by the graveside and showing them what to do brought a knot in my throat. When I got back to the office, I had tears in my eyes; I still can't believe Maxwell was no more. Life!!What a way to start the day and a new week. And oh! I just remembered I forgot to pay for the kids' feeding fees for the week. Jesus! Take the wheel!

16th May: I went to the cemetery to check on the flowers, and they had planted it. Walking out of the cemetery, I said to myself," I can't believe I can freely walk in and out of a cemetery like I'm walking in and out of a house." Life has a way of making you adjust to change. Now, I could foresee these visits as a cycle that may never end. Why? When the boys grow up enough to understand everything, I will have to tell them every detail and show them where their father was buried. "Tears in my eyes, hands shaking and heart beating, I just sighted the final arrangements for the One Year Anniversary of Maxwell's demise. I forwarded to my contacts, and the reality hit me, making me once again sorrowful". God has a way of sending people to uplift you. A senior colleague walked into my office that same day and told me that Maxwell would be happy to know that I am keeping well and taking good care of the boys but won't be happy to know that I am not surviving, that I am even finding ways to kill myself, that I'm being diagnosed with heart diseases and head problems. He said life is war and that peace only comes to obstruct the war for just a season. Therefore when bad things happen, we should know that it is normal. This man had continuously told me that if I don't take care of myself, no one would. I have even broken down in tears several times in front of him while he was telling me to take care of myself. Thank God for senior colleagues in the workspace like his type. I will not forget the one who also tells me not to allow the situation to cause me to coil up and lose confidence. It is simply not easy; this burden, this weight, this task ahead!

17th May: Driving to work, listening to Sunny FM, and the song they were playing was by Karen Peck- Four Day's

Late. The song recounts how Lazarus' sisters told Jesus he was late because their brother was dead. Nevertheless, Jesus still raised their brother. When we think God is too late in our situation and all hope is lost, he is still on time because his ways are not our ways. My mind went back to the night of 29th May 2017 and how I prayed that God would intervene and keep Maxwell safe and alive. I believed that even if he were dead and He wanted to raise him, He would. I had tears in my eyes thinking about it, and I managed to hold them back.

I went over to the graveside to add more flowers for planting before going to the office.

On my way back from work, I told myself that I miss Maxwell, I miss our closeness, I miss us waking up at dawn to chat and just laugh. I miss us dancing in the room. I miss us chasing each other around. I miss him standing by me and making conversations in the kitchen while I cooked. I miss him shouting my name with excitement, "Beeeee," when he came back from work, and he knew I was home preparing something or experimenting with weird recipes. I missed squeezing oranges for him; I missed him asking us what we would eat late in the night when he knew we had had supper and he just wanted some pancakes or 'kelewele' to add on. I missed our walks in the area… I MISS YOU, MAXWELL.

The truth of the matter is that it is very hard to believe that you are no more, although the evidence is there.

22nd May: I personally watered the flowers at the graveside and did this every morning. It gave me some relief. Some weeks later, I was told that planting flowers by Maxwell's graveside is not a great achievement that I wanted to inform everyone.

Note that when you are down, and people feel you are not down enough according to their standards, they would like to push you down further. Expect anything and everything while you grieve.

24th May: Another court hearing, the headlines, as usual, were making my heart skip beats. I was asking myself if this will ever end. Feeling tired of the insensitivities as the court proceedings may seem, I told myself that I will wait for the next hearing on 5th June.

28th May: I took a trip to the cemetery to water the flowers and came home very sad. I cried a lot throughout the day, but I also occupied myself with activities in my shop. Maxwell's aunty Martha came around because she called and heard me crying. She rushed from work to come and spend time with me. God bless her.

29th May: It was a long day filled with activities. Church Service in the morning, Trust fund was launched, and a sod-cutting ceremony for the monument was done. During the wreath laying, I kept staring at the grave. Life is short; life is fleeting. Nothing is permanent. Today we are here, tomorrow, we are gone. We are like a puff of smoke.

30th May: I woke up, played some worship medleys, dressed up, dropped the boys in school, and headed to the office. I didn't want to stay home and be sad.

2nd June: A chaplain in Burma Camp fixed a widowhood stoppage meeting with me. She prayed, removed my rings, and we ended with a chat. I came home thereafter.

3rd June: Thanksgiving service went on, followed by a reception. During the service at the Catholic Church in Burma Camp, the priest prayed for me. He mentioned that Maxwell and I had no spiritual connection again. Hearing those words were painful; such a forceful separation caused by death. Reception was filled with drama, but it ended all the same.

4th June: Paid a courtesy call on the President with the family to show our appreciation. The day ended on a bad note.

5th June: On my way to drop the boys at school, I received unpalatable messages, which were enough to crush my spirit. A few of the insults had to do with my inability to organise a reception because I can't even organise my home, and various insults about my parents and my entire family, concluding that my family is full of ungrateful people. What I know is that, my family is full of people who simply mind their business. They would never hurt a fly. They may not have material wealth, but they have respect for human beings. These messages were unfounded and uncalled for, but I came to understand that the messages were sent to break me and force me into some sort of subjection, but since I had decided I was above this drama, I refused to give more power to the sender. I simply ignored the messages. I have mastered the art of ignoring messages, even to the surprise of my friends, who can't stand Facebook messages that seek to denigrate me. According to the message, I have become ungrateful and disrespectful after becoming famous through Maxwell's death. I was accused of painting a wrong picture about my marriage which in reality wasn't (I don't remember either granting a press conference on my marriage or telling the world how perfect my marriage had been). If I can summarise how my marriage was, we've done beach walks, we've sat under trees to share wine, we've taken walks holding hands, we've danced together in the room alone, in front of our kids and at functions, we've chased each other around, we've played like kids, we've even played scrabble in our free time, we've planned for the future and pictured good life together, we've fought over strange numbers calling at odd hours, we've been there for each other in our difficult moments, we've offered our shoulders to each other to cry. To put it simply, we had great times together, much as we had struggles like any other marriage, but I would rather trumpet the good times because our good times were more than the bad times.

My so-called impending failed marriage was going to be caused by my over-possessiveness. Welcome to Ghana, where a marriage collapses, and it's solely the fault of what the woman did or did not do. Oh, she can't keep a man, as if men are commodities; oh, she can't take care of her home, oh, she can't bathe her children, oh, this, oh, that.

Dear sister, be delivered from unnecessary guilt and unpleasant tags because your marriage failed. Live and live. Certainly, do your best. Certainly, love wholly. Certainly, go the extra mile. Certainly, do not allow society to hang the cross of a failed marriage around your neck only.

These messages were the tip of the iceberg in terms of all the accusations and insinuations I suffered after my loss. It was reported to me how a friend's daughter was on admission at Korle Bu, where she heard another woman whose daughter was also on admission talk about how I didn't love my husband enough to have maintained my hair uncut. My friend retorted by saying that it's not compulsory because sometimes, some widows pay fines instead of cutting their hair. The lady insisted that I should have cut my hair as proof of my love. I guess she didn't know that cutting my hair was never part of any discussion. She moved on to take a swipe at why I still kept Mahama as my surname. She wondered, is it that I don't have a surname or what? I started thinking about the days Maxwell suggested I add my surname to the Mahama name. I always told him that I didn't like the way it would sound- Barbara Botchwey Mahama, then he would say I should do it Barbara B. Mahama. I always told him it was fine to just use the Barbara Mahama. He is gone now and would not be able to prove that I insisted on not adding my maiden name. Let me blow my own horn, oh yes. I am a builder and not a destroyer; I don't take things to destroy. I don't go into people's lives to scatter things and split up families. I am a daughter of God. Genuine souls are proud to have me in their corner because they see beyond the surface. A pure soul is a pure soul. I know who I am, and no one can convince me that I am who I am not. Wherever that woman is, I hope she at least acknowledges that I have tried to uphold the name in the best way I can.

Is it worth marrying with so much hope, loving with your all, sacrificing and being there for the man you married, and then when he's dead and gone, the world thinks you never contributed anything to his life because obviously, you didn't enter the marriage with your own luxury cars, money and wealth? A woman's contribution is always overlooked, and oh! It would be your fellow women who pour such venom on you, sometimes to your face.

Women always want to feel better than other women, but it's high time we realise that we don't have to compete with one another because there is room for everyone to shine. I can even decide to hold my torch to light up your path for you, and it's fine; I don't have to use it to insult you. I don't have to expect you to reciprocate, and I don't have to burden your life by letting you think you are indebted to me forever because of a kind gesture.

My Personal Nuggets of Wisdom

Reflections

The empowered 21st-century woman is capable of taking care of herself and her children when her husband dies.

The empowered 21st-century woman should be equipped with knowledge and skills that would help her to survive in case of unexpected death of her husband.

The empowered 21st-century widow does not have to rush into another marriage after her husband dies in order to be catered for by another man.

The 21st-century woman is not so weak that she cannot take care of her own children after her husband dies.

The truth is that women have always been strong, and they have been capable of taking care of their own affairs.

Also, know that:

1.   Grieving is an individual thing, and no one can really help you except God and yourself. Try not to appear broken for approval because those who expect you to look broken cannot fix your brokenness. Take one day at a time; everything stems from the inside, so it's very private. Win from within. Gather momentum from within and shine. You alone know how you feel.

2.   Because we can do all things through Christ who strengthens us, we can divide ourselves into so many pieces. A part feeling hopeless and lost; a part feeling weak; a part feeling strong with hope and faith; a part wanting to hold on because of the many people whose lives depend on us. Grieving is actually going mad without necessarily being or looking mad.

3.   No one came into this world with a manuscript and a map. We don't know tomorrow, we just have to be grateful for today and enjoy it, and if tomorrow comes, you better be grateful and enjoy it.

4.   In everything, give thanks and never lose trust in the big God up there because he knows your tomorrow, and you can bet on it that, He has your good at heart. All things will work together for your good.

5.   People like to talk about tradition when it suits them. They never talk about tradition in its entirety. I'm for a culture that pats a widow on the shoulder to tell her kudos for looking into the face of an adversary and not shaking. I'm for the culture that tells a widow she is doing well by holding her head up and doing excellent.

6.   As a 21st-century woman, be ready to enrich yourself from all angles so that you are not found wanting when the

evil day comes. You must have something to show and something to lean on... something more than beauty.

7. Always remember that time flies really fast. Don't be too obsessed with the problems that you refuse to make plans to achieve.

8. Every stage of your life has lessons to be learnt, be open-minded.

9. Be patient with your learning process; feel free to make mistakes but don't let your mistakes cripple you and put you in a shell. Keep moving.

10. There is light at the end of the tunnel, and you should not lose hope.

11. Avoid people who want to be babied, each one for himself; nobody should be a burden on anybody saddled with kids and struggling to stay sane after a loss.

12. Don't let your pain make you a pain in people's lives.

13. It is important to come to the realisation that you've been hurt and you need time to heal in order to be whole again. It will be a long process but trust the process.

14. Healing is a daily affair; waking up and deciding you need healing is the first part of the process.

15. You can't be on the journey of healing and constantly open up yourself for people to hurt you. No matter who they are, do not allow them.

Finding Courage to Press On and Move Forward

There must be a conscious effort to gather the courage to press on after you lose a loved one. We move forward and not necessarily move on. We live side by side with the effects of the loss, but we find a way to take the power the effect has over us. We refuse to be crippled by the loss, not because the loss wasn't painful but because we've found the courage to press on in all of this. We can easily lose ourselves in despair and hopelessness. I'm keeping busy with my career and other things I have ventured into. We should immortalise the memory of our loved ones by standing strong. We should immortalise the memory of our loved ones by excelling and being successful at what we do, and that is only possible if there is a will to live and push through. I'm living, I'm taking one day at a time, and my favorite social activity now is hanging out with the children.

During my moments of grief, I found solace in God's word, God's anointed vessels, some angels in disguise, and some creative actions I took.

One of the few activities that brought relief to me was giving. Sometimes helping people is such a relief, so I decided to up my giving game. Maxwell and I used to discuss how it would be nice if, in the near future, we could be of help to families who needed medical interventions for their sick children, among others. He also wanted to take up youth empowerment, especially youth entrepreneurship. We saw ourselves putting smiles on people's faces. We had plans.

Secondly, I invested time into exercise. Let me not underestimate the importance of exercise in this journey. I have found that I enjoyed the dance classes. I used to do aerobics before the incident, and I loved it. However, in this journey, the aerobics classes, the dance classes, the yoga classes, and the treadmill gave me a different meaning. When the pain from the exercise is felt, I challenge myself to do more, fight harder, and not to give up. Exercise to me now means persevering and smiling after the storm. I found cooking therapeutic as well, so every meal I made had meaning for me.

I found solace in friends who came around to mourn, served, and slept over to keep me company. They combined work with school and taking care of the boys and me. They fixed jollof days. They cried, they laughed, and they felt my pain but tried to hide it so I will be cheerful.

There were friends who were not residing in Ghana but registered their presence in my heart with their constant checking in and touching base. Maxwell left me some great friends from his side. I never knew most of them until after the incident, but they stuck like glue. Thank God for friends who stick closer than brothers. They have been friends indeed. God bless them!

God Sends Help

God will cause strangers to help you. I have lived that scripture, and I'm still living that scripture. First of all, I started getting calls from people far away in different countries wanting to pray with me. The concern and love in their voices were unexplainable. I still have people who call and pray with me. People send me encouraging messages day in and day out. Two ladies actually made it a task to call me first thing in the morning every day to pray with me. There were times their calls came minutes apart because they were in the same time zone. The great development that has emerged out of this is the fact that we are like sisters now, and we chat almost every day. One also called and arranged for sewn clothes to be brought to me to wear. One wanted to pay for my groceries every month. These are young ladies who decided to pour themselves out and help heal a fellow sister.

Not forgetting the Go Fund Me organisers who were so passionate and still are about my issues. The strangers from near who also made contact were warm and comforting. There was one who provided drinks for the boys enough to last them a whole year. She used to come to us in the evenings with bags of KFC meals, and sometimes we just sat in her car talking about nothing. Now I call her mummy and she is so protective over me and the kids. She just wanted to make sure we were okay. One day, she thought my braids were old and made sure to let her hairdressers ambush me and take out the braids, and an appointment was fixed to re-braid. How could I forget the one whose dad was too worried about me that he was forced to come look for me and make sure we were okay. He still shows us kindness. The constant checking in and the conscious effort to let me know that I need to take care of myself is much appreciated.

I don't want to attempt mentioning names because I always realise I have tons of people I communicate with on a daily basis now that I didn't know before. That is how God can use strangers to comfort you during difficult situations.

You showed love and kindness to a widow, and her children, and God will reward you immensely. I could decide to write a lovely book from the emails I received on a daily basis and still receive.

Not forgetting the family members who left their comfortable beds to come and sleep on that hard floor just to make sure I was okay and took all the insults they got in good faith. Not forgetting the in-laws who kept coming and making sure there was stuff at home etc. I appreciate my church family who came to clean up, stand by and avail themselves to run errands for the visitors. The meaningful hugs and the unspoken words from family members who were as broken as I was can never be forgotten.

I can never forget the kindness of the kids' proprietress, aunty Sheila. You've been a shield and you've made this journey bearable. God bless you.

Caution

In the midst of kind gestures from people, there are others that may not live up to expectations or may not fulfill the promises uttered. Calls may be ignored; your matter may be shoved under the table but remember that whoever is supposed to be in your life will be. Therefore, to minimise disappointment when grieving, take promises as mere sayings. If they come to pass, thank God but be quick to move on if they don't come true. Make plans, have a focus, have timelines, and just take it as if your support system is no more, but you still have to make things work. Everyone is busy with their issues, so no one will leave their family matters to attend to yours. The best they would do is juggle your matters in addition to their personal matters, and you have to know that one matter must be sacrificed for the other, and it would definitely be yours. Don't expect too much.

While Waiting

While you wait to see what God has in store for you, while you wait on God to see how the next stage of your life will unfold according to HIS plan, it is important to:

- Enjoy your own company.
- Celebrate yourself.
- Spend time with yourself, gift yourself.
- Everything you would want people to do for you, do them for yourself. You want flowers, buy yourself flowers. Take yourself out. Enter a dessert shop and eat ice cream.
- Read books.
- Further your education.
- Gather knowledge.
- Love yourself.
- Bask in positive affirmations about your life.
- Dream big, put pen and paper down, and write your dreams and where you want to see yourself.
- Go out with friends when you feel like.
- Don't belittle yourself, and don't feel nothing good will come out of your life.
- Invest in knowing your worth. Invest in knowing who you really are and what you really want.

- Grow and mature from your experiences.
- Exude positivity and spread love.
- Create money-making avenues- a woman's best protection is a little money of her own.

Looking back, I realise I always did something on the side; I have never been an idle person. I have been full of ideas. In primary school, I helped my mother sell powdered soap by deciding to have a spot in the Dome market, at the time when the market was at the rail station. Also, in primary school, I decided to sell oranges, and I did. I've sold doughnuts in school made by my mum also. While I waited for university admission, I helped prophecy mum run her fashion house, and I had about 13 workers to oversee; I was in charge of quality control.

In university, I sold packed fruits; I went to Agbogbloshie market early morning on Saturdays and bought the fruits, woke up every morning to wash and prep them, and packed them in their beautiful packs. I sealed them with beautifully designed stickers on. The business was named Bibi Fruits. Also, when Jaden was three months old, I sold hot dogs at Zenith college. The sewing business wasn't my first attempt at business. I have tried selling children's diaries that I made myself etc. In short, get busy, and attempt great things. Make a name for yourself; make a mark for yourself. What should people know you for?

A Child's Emotions

Maxwell's death affected the boys differently. For Jaden, the crowd that gathered and the activities fascinated him. He used the opportunity to throw tantrums, and he became addicted to games. Immediately he saw a visitor, he drew near and asked for his or her phone, so he could play games.

Jerry was distant; he was confused and was only two years at the time. He had temperatures often during the early days of the death, and he preferred to be quiet and keep to himself, only accepting to go to a few known people compared to Jaden, who was jumping from one person to the other just because he was interested in taking their phones.

The bucket of Maxwell's pick-up was a source of joy for the boys when Maxwell was alive because he always played with them inside. They had memories of it that I may not know the details of because their playtime in daddy's pick-up mostly happened in my absence. They expected to see the pick-up parked at the usual parking space, and when they stopped seeing it, they would ask where their father's pick-up was. When we step out, and they see soldiers in pick-ups, they argue among themselves because the little one would say that is their dad in the pick-up, and the elder boy would say that is not the colour of the pick-up, so that can't be their dad. Oftentimes, we overlook the fact that a loss affects the children also. We forget that they are also trying to process the whole thing without being able to express it. They have their fears and their thoughts too. When you find yourself among selfish people, a child's emotions and well-being would easily be forgotten. The grown-ups want to be babied, and the burden is on the widow.

The first day they had swimming lessons with their school's swimming team, they told me that they swam in the pool their father used to swim in, and they were right. I didn't think they would remember such things.

Spending time alone with the boys means so much to me because I get to connect and bond with them in a way that is unexplainable. I get to sense their fears and listen to their conversations. In a way, we encourage ourselves and get to tell ourselves that we are in this together, although we never voice it out. I see the concern in their eyes, and when they ask me whether I am okay, it always feels like it is Maxwell asking me how I am faring.

To date, both boys deal with the situation in their own way. The first one has everything bottled up. Sometimes I feel he is disappointed in his dad for not returning. Recently, I had to sit him down to tell him that his dad would have loved to come back, but we don't always get what we want, and we need to learn to live all the same.

I have realised that whereas the second boy can watch a movie and not be affected by death scenes, the first boy is not able to handle death scenes at all. As grown-ups have triggers that open the floodgates of grief, children also have their own triggers, and we may never know if we don't make a conscious effort to know and support them.

There was a time when the World Wars were a topic in the first boy's class, and that caused a serious trigger for him to the extent that his teacher had to take him out of the class to calm him down. When I heard this, I became so sad and asked him to tell me how he felt when the topic was raised. He opened up and told me that he missed his father, and he broke down crying. The tears came deep from the heart. The kind that shakes you. I still get those kinds of tears sometimes. I tried to calm him down, but I ended up crying more than him. One of the unpleasant feelings in this life is seeing your child struggle to come to terms with a difficult situation, and you wish their pain is transferred to you, but as little as they are, that is an experience they also have to go through. Sometimes the little one also misses his dad and tells me he is sad his dad isn't around. We try as much as possible to recount the beautiful times they had with their dad so they have enough happy memories to keep them going. As the grief journey is a rollercoaster one for adults, it is same for children. So yes, sometimes my boys only want to talk about their heroic dad, and other times, they want to talk about how they feel about his absence. They have asked me whether they can visit their father's grave in the near future, and I told them yes. They are brave little boys who are dealing with the absence of their father. There is this big cross they are carrying on their young shoulders that I wish they didn't have to carry, but God knows best. I am very proud of them now, and I am even prouder of what they will turn out to be because God is jealously watching over them.

We move forward because the pain of a loss never goes away. We just learn to live with it and make sure it doesn't hold us in bondage, fear, or limit us.

Single Parenting

Single parenting is a new thing to me, and I've found myself tossing ideas in my mind trying to figure out the best approach to bringing up children who have become fatherless at such a young age. I keep telling myself that the initial years are the crucial ones, and my attitude towards this loss will either affect the boys negatively or positively. Would they want to see a mother who is always broken and helpless, or would they want to see a mother who exudes positivity and strength? When a loved one dies, and there are little children left behind, efforts should be made by all and sundry to protect them from the effects of the loss as much as possible. The surviving spouse should know that it's his or her full responsibility to shield the children. Other family members can help here and there, but the children are your responsibility. You are alive for a reason so take charge. See God as your co-parent. Entrust your children in His care because He knows them better than you do, and His eyes will always watch over them, whereas your eyes as a parent won't be everywhere.

Galatians 5:22-23 always comes to mind when I think about the best way to bring the boys up, so I want to share with you so that together, we can make conscious efforts to shield our children from grief and cushion them a bit. We don't want broken children growing into broken adults.

Fruits of the Spirit Parenting

Love: I feel that it is important for parents to show love to their children by showing love to people around them without discrimination. The little ones learn from how we relate to people. I wouldn't want my boys to grow up and see a mother who suddenly turned bitter and aggressive towards people around her, especially to domestic help. It's not difficult to love your own child, so if you want to show your child what love is, demonstrate it by relating to people well. Love without discrimination, do not love based on the colour of the skin and do not love only a certain class of people. Just love. People who can't love lack the Holy Spirit because it is the Holy Spirit who gives the fruit of love. Some people cannot also receive love. When you give love, and you receive love, you make life bearable for yourself and for people around you, including your children. Now I have the duty of showering them with love and showering them with the love their father would have showered them with. In grief, you can still be able to love and protect the little ones that need it the most. Avail yourself to be a tool of love. May our children not say, "My father/mother died, and my surviving parent couldn't love and protect us, so we were left at the mercy of people". You are alive for a reason. You are alive for your children to fulfill their destinies. Guide them.

Joy: This is important to me because growing up, we didn't have much. The times my mother was joyful and could lead us to sing all manner of songs and even play games with us were cherished moments. She was a nursery teacher, and we sometimes turned our house into a nursery school. Maxwell told me one day that he liked the fact that I am always cheerful, and he got used to my cheerful nature, so much so that he complained anytime I appeared moody due to tiredness or another issue. He liked a happy wife and wanted our children to grow up in a happy environment. I personally saw how Jaden's face lit up anytime Maxwell and I had a little dance time or chasing each other around time.

Now that their father is no more, will I choose being moody over being happy? Will they be happy in a moody environment? Will they know what a happy home is if I decide to always be sad? What environment would Maxwell have wanted for his kids to grow up in? When you have the Holy Spirit, you have unspeakable joy. People may say you don't have any worries in life because they don't know that the joy God gives is forever. Joy is a fruit of the spirit. Even in pain, you can have joy, which would baffle the naysayers. Ask God for Joy.

Peace: The peace God gives us cannot be disturbed by the worries of life. When God gives you something, he gives it to you. The trials may come, the tribulations may come, but God's peace will give you a certain outlook. You will be calm in the storm. You will not fret; you will not accuse people of things they haven't done because your mind is busily cooking up stories. You will relax, relax, and relax. You will watch the problems unfold, but the peace of God will tell you that the problems will not last. People who exude peace may be seen as fools and not "wild" people, so they cannot achieve anything in life. A parent who has peace will have a sound mind to bring up his or her children in a way that pleases God. What will fretting and rushing do? I choose peace. Ask God for peace. When you lose a loved one, you need peace to be able to face the task ahead when there are children involved. Be ready to show people who cannot give you peace the exit. They will say you have changed but know that you cannot trade the change that is necessary for your sanity for all the approval of men.

Long-suffering: Patience or long-suffering is also a fruit of the spirit. Impatience can break relationships. Give your children the room to express themselves and teach them patience and tolerance. Teach them to be accommodating and teach them to give people a chance to explain themselves. Ask God for patience because his timings are not our timings, and without patience, we can never understand his ways. In difficult times, do not let your impatience break the bond you can have with your children.

Kindness: I choose to be kind because I want my children to grow up being kind. I want them to be kind to people and not rub it in their faces. I want them to be kind to people without expecting any allegiance. I want them to know that kindness is an opportunity and a blessing to the one showing it. Show your children that showing kindness is a privilege because a time comes when you would wish, above all else, to get the opportunity to show a little kindness, but it may be too late.

Goodness, faithfulness, gentleness, and self-control are the rest of the fruits of the spirit. Parents need to show goodness towards neighbours. Do good and not evil, and show faithfulness in every aspect of their life, like being faithful employees, faithful children of God, the list goes on. Show your children that faithfulness is a lifetime decision, and you don't just decide to forfeit your faithfulness to God because you faced challenges. Show gentleness at all times instead of being aggressive and always barking. Why should your children fear you to the extent that they can't be themselves when they are with you? Why can't they have opinions? Why should everyone around you be jittery? Why should the atmosphere around you be tensed? Exercise self-control. Emotions must be controlled, not necessarily suppressed. You need to know when to throw tantrums and when not to.

It is my wish that parents exhibit the fruits of the spirit so that the children grow up in a loving and peaceful environment. We don't need troubled children who will grow up to be troubled youths and adults and then troubled leaders. God help us.

Events that inspired me to take a stand for myself and the kids were mainly from the dreams I had after the loss:

➢ Sudden deaths come with sudden or rude awakenings, and this reality may crop up in dreams. In my case, I expected Maxwell to offer help in my dreams, and when it appeared he was unconcerned, I got confused and became angry.

➢ One instance is when I dreamt and saw myself and the boys in a pit, and Maxwell was outside looking down at us. I suggested to him to come and get us out, and he just stood there, not doing anything. I was shocked and became angry.

➢ Another instance is when I saw him drive past a junction I was standing at with the boys, I expected him to stop, and he didn't. I chased him and made sure he stopped so I could question him. I asked whether he didn't see us standing there to approach us, and he said he was going home. I wondered what he meant by he was going home when home is where the kids and I are. In that dream, I was ready to announce to the world that Maxwell never died, as everyone thinks. I was very pleased with myself in the dream because I felt that I was right all along, that Maxwell would come back to us. Anytime I woke up from such dreams, the realisation hit me more that I needed to stand up for myself and the boys. So I decided to stand up for myself. I drew strength from God's word, and inspiration from the dream pattern to arise and face all the challenges lined up for my new status.

Spiritual Battles

In a perfect world, after the loss of the head of the house, partner, or parent, there should be rest for the grieving parties. Unfortunately, this is far from reality in this wicked world we find ourselves in. I have come to really understand the verse in the Bible that says the devil came to kill, steal, and destroy. You are sometimes plunged into constant spiritual battles because there is a fight for your sanity, your peace, your joy, and anything and anyone that makes you happy. Forces are joined to conspire and make sure you never recover from an affliction, but in all, know that God never forsakes His own, and he has said that affliction shall not happen twice. Don't stop praying and seeking God's face. Fully trust in His perfect will.

Today, I lay bare some of the things that have been thrown at me so that when you find yourself in a similar situation, you would know you are not the first person to go through this. We can only pray that we don't become bitter people and make life unbearable for the younger generation coming up. We strive to be the generation that went through hell and shields the next generation from going through hell. It is well.

In summary:

- People have wished me dead.

- People have wished my children dead.

- People have wished that I keep experiencing pain upon pain upon pain.

- People have stood in places to the hearing of others and cursed me openly because they feel I have wronged them by my actions or inactions as a widow.

When people are deep in bitterness, and they openly show their hatred for you, they would want all the bad things they desire for you to come to pass. Should I say they will watch over their words, making sure they come to pass? But there is a higher authority who is also watching over His words in your life to perform them. The one who has said be strong and courageous, the one who has said be still and know that I am God, the one who has said His plans for you are that of good and not evil. May God's plan for your life overrule that of wicked people around you. Refuse to be a tool to be used by the devil to destroy your fellow human being. The reward for this is unpleasant; you simply cannot fight God, you cannot curse whom God has blessed, and you cannot touch God's anointed.

Highlights of Years Three To Five

Year Two (2019)

In the second year, I didn't write much, but I will attempt to summarise the year for you. I had more crying moments this year; it was as if the reality of the loss was now hitting me. I would be up in the middle of the night crying. I had pastor friends all over the world who were ever ready to say a prayer with me during my down moments, and to date, I call them to pray with me when I feel a rush of emotions and I break down to cry.

This year was when I decided I can't keep being a carpet for people to walk on me. I decided it was not okay to just sit and allow people to look down on me, no matter who they were. There comes a time when you need to say enough is enough. There comes a time when you need to choose yourself. I was accused of burning bridges this year, but what use is a bridge that is unreliable and only causes you pain? This year, attempts were made to twist every word I said and every action of mine.

This year was when Maxwell's monument was unveiled. I will never forget the day of the unveiling ceremony because as I made my way to the grounds where everyone was seated, I bumped into a grandmother on a bridge. I had this wide smile on my face (I can be crying and still smile) to greet her, and she returned my smile with hot red eyes that screamed, "Get lost; I hate you." I don't know what my crime was, I don't know what she felt I had done, but this woman, this elderly woman, met a young widow who was hurting and decided to show hatred.

I decided that it was pointless trying to please people. I wasn't going to update anybody about anything concerning my children and me, and I wasn't about to spend sleepless nights wondering why someone had decided to hate me. I decided that it is very okay to be the bad person in the picture so far as my sanity is intact. I wasn't going to fret about who was talking ill about me to people, and I had no desire to prove a point. Simply put, I had no desire to try and change perceptions and to try and explain myself. I told myself that I can't control what people choose to say about me, and I can't control what people choose to hear and believe about me.

In the latter part of 2019, the devil came knocking on my door. I boldly told him/her/it to get out. We had an experience that changed our lives. A scary experience. An experience that scares a child and deprives him of his sleep. An experience that keeps a mother up at night to watch her child sleep. An experience that keeps a mother up at night to war and seek God's face. An experience that saw men of God such as Bishop Eddy Addy, Bishop Fabin, Reverend Eastwood Anaba, Bishop Aryee, and many other pastors who were like family stand in the gap for my children and me. In 2019, I asked myself, "Whose report will you believe." One of the boys had an attack; I had to make a decision, a painful decision, to choose to put him on lifelong medication. Those who were really close to me know this, those who paid for MRIs and other tests, and those who decided to let their personal doctors assess the situation, thank you!

I was a confused mother; I asked God questions, where from this at this time? As I keep saying, when a situation is new to me, although I fret inside, I appear very calm outside. I had to meet with pediatricians because I needed to understand the situation fully before making a decision. I needed to ask all the questions. On one of the days before meeting with the pediatrician, I had to pick up a test result, and I opened it and saw what the diagnosis was. I may have shed a few tears, but I gathered the courage to tell the doctor I was on my way to her office and that I had opened the report. She waited for me; we started chatting, and I broke down in tears. She looked at me and said I was a strong woman to have been able to open the report, call her to tell her, and drive to her in a calm manner. I told her I needed time to make a decision, and she agreed.

We kept praying. Sunday after Sunday, when we close from church, we will spend time in Bishop Addy's office, and before we leave, he would pray with us and anoint us and assure us everything will be fine. All the men of God mentioned above, and those not mentioned, would constantly call and pray with us, visit us, and anoint us.

2019 ended with uncertainties without me knowing what path I wanted to choose and what decision I was sticking with regarding this new disturbing development.

People are fighting silent battles you know nothing of; stop making life unbearable for those around you. Live and let others live.

Year Three (2020)

We started 2020 with an unsolved burden. We tried to stay happy as a family with a lot of activities and enjoying one another's company. Usual routines such as friends coming over and such continued, but silently, I was battling with this decision I hadn't yet taken. I wondered whether I was doing the right thing. I still had my breaking down moments, and I really wondered whether there will be a whole year where there won't be breaking down moments.

One experience I will never forget in this year is that one night, a naughty cat decided to disturb my sleep. The cat kept crying behind my window. I thought it was my landlady's cat, so I overlooked it. For hours, the cat was still by my window crying and crying, so finally, I had to open the window and attempt to sack the cat. The cat left my window, and I had some peace of mind. I woke up later to run some errands, I got to my first point, which was a salon, and I could hear a cat crying. I got to the second point, which was a supermarket, and I still heard a cat crying. I said to myself that I was having a strange day full of cat cries. I got to my third point later in the day, which was an apartment building I wanted us to move into, and lo and behold, there was a cat crying.

I came out, and the security man alerted me that a cat was crying from inside my car, and he suspected that he was stuck in my bonnet. We opened the bonnet, and we could hear the cat crying but couldn't locate where it was, so I had to take the car to a shell shop for some parts to be removed in an attempt to release the cat. The mechanics were shocked. What is more shocking is the fact that a cat transitioned from crying by my window to entering my car. There were many cars on the compound, but the cat moved from my window and entered my car. When the mechanics, after many tries, finally succeeded in removing the cat, the cat came out behaving in a weird manner and later dying without being touched.

Strange things happen, and although many times we try not to read meanings into occurrences, some are too strange to ignore.

In this year, I decided to agree for my son to be on medication. I prayed one morning, told God to guide me in this decision, and asked that His perfect will be done. I took the prescription, put it in my bag, and went to a pharmacy to ask for the price of the medicine. I knew the medicine off my head because almost every night, I google it to read about it, so I didn't need to take the prescription out to know the name. I asked of the drug, and I was told the price. I said God, really? Is this the path you want me to be on, an expensive drug for a prolonged time that would have to be bought many times in a month? God, you know I don't need this stress at this time of my life. I told the pharmacist I needed to look at the prescription to get the dosage I needed. I opened my bag, and the prescription was nowhere to be found. I went into my car to search and search, and I couldn't find it. I came home to search; I searched under my bed and everywhere and still couldn't find it. I said God if this is a sign, let your will be done. I was at peace from that day.

There were still instances where the scary situation tried to rear its head, but like a storm, we always saw it passing. That year, Maxwell's 3rd anniversary fell on a working day. I woke up very early in the morning and dropped my wreaths, and went to work.

In the latter part of the year, I decided to take a leap of faith. I wanted to build a place of worship for God in honour of Maxwell. I told God that I want to build a small church, and He should look at it to release certain things that have delayed in my life. It felt as if people were deliberately preventing me from receiving things that were due me. People felt I didn't deserve certain things. I needed a drastic intervention from God. People like playing God, and people like to be stopcocks in your life.

Year 4 (2021)

In the fourth year, I had an eight-year-old son. The reality of raising the children single-handedly sunk in. The fact that they look up to me for every support sunk in. I still had my breaking down moments, and the shocking thing was the fact that the pain still felt fresh and so the intensity of the cry hadn't changed. The triggers had reduced, and so when I heard certain words which were unbearable in the beginning, I just became indifferent now.

In this year, the church building was completed, and it was dedicated. Immediately it was completed, a major prayer was answered by God. God gave me a valuable gift that made the cost of the church building look like a drop of water in the ocean. God used a great woman to bless me and answer my prayers. Thank you, mum. I also told God that the place of worship should serve as a neutralising effect against every attack the enemy decides to throw at my children and me. I wanted an altar that would speak for my children and me and my unborn generation.

For the Eighth-year birthday celebration, I decided to make a prayer book that had prayers from about sixteen seasoned men of God in it. I want to be able to let the boys know that they can always trust God. I want them to grow knowing that there is God and He cares. It was a beautiful little project.

In this year also, I had to prepare to change locations for work. I was embracing growth; I was embracing change; I was embracing being independent; I was discovering myself more and more. I got to the new location without the kids so I could prepare for their joining me. Being apart from them wasn't easy, but in this journey, we all learn to adjust. They were fine because I left them in capable hands.

When they finally joined me, we were one big family. I saw how quickly they had grown within a short period of time in my absence. The joy of their joining was tampered with when, exactly a week after they joined me, this unpleasant situation that we've put behind us and sort of closed the chapter on reared its head. I said God, not again, in this place. Prayers went up, and hospital appointments were booked. The first doctor who attended to us took his time to ask about the history of the situation and did his assessments. Further tests were done. Thorough tests were done, and he decided to discharge us and assure us that it was nothing. There was no need for medications, and there was no need for panic, and he's sure it has passed, never to return again.

Later, another doctor decided to take up the case and book us in; we attended the normal appointments. To the glory of God, we go to appointments just for going sake so that all parties involved will be convinced that all is well. There is a God who rules in the affairs of men, and this God has done me good. He has loved me and treasured me.

Year 5 (2022)

In this fifth year, I feel light; I keep taking stock of events over the past years. I am at peace. God is protecting the kids and me jealously. There are attacks from the pit of hell that

God shows to me through dreams and through prayers. I am not perfect, but I have gotten assurance from God that His mercies are new every morning. God has promised me that He has my interest at heart. He has promised to be with me, and He has reminded me that I should not be afraid.

In May 2022, I kept thinking about how I wanted to mark Maxwell's fifth year, and I kept sensing peace, and I saw a dove in my mind's eye. I then decided to have a dove release. I googled what it meant and where I could book for one, and it was as if God was in sync with me; finding one wasn't difficult at all. I did the release a week before the 29th, and when I released the dove, I started crying. I cried my heart out.

I was letting go and letting God. I was releasing all the bottled-up emotions, pain, confusion, etc. I was opening up myself for God's next move in my life. When we came home after the release, it was as if the tears had decided to flow like a river; one of my pastor friends called to pray with me, and I never stopped crying. Five years? These emotions have a way of shocking me.

On 29th May, I woke up brave and strong and went to church. During the service, I alerted one of the singers that my husband died five years ago, and I'm feeling sad, so I would appreciate it if the church prays with me. She alerted one of the elders who raised the topic and told the church to stretch their hands towards me and lift me up in prayers. I cried like a baby! When the prayers stopped, I felt as if a heavy load had been lifted off me. I felt free. This is a new church in my new location, where the people do not know me at all, but they joined hands to lift me up. The Holy Spirit isn't bound to any location; he appears at the right places when he's called. Call him and experience him for yourself. He's sweet and his influence is marvelous.

Emails from Admirers

29th July, 2017

A gloomy day it was.............

It was a busy day for me as I had piled work on my desk from the previous day; these files needed my urgent attention. Therefore, the group discussion supported with evidence from the social media was not in any way attractive to me. I managed to sign off these files and dated them, 30th May 2017.

Now I was free, so I enquired of my colleagues, the subject of their earlier discussion which I was reluctantly told due to my indifferent attitude earlier in the day. I declined to look at the evidence because I wasn't too interested.

Discovering that the widow was a sister!

After lunch that day, I visited Facebook and saw a testimony the victim of the unfortunate incident had written about his lovely wife which had already gone viral. I read the post more than five times and I realized the lady was one of us!! She was one of daddy's girls! There was this sudden gloom that rained on me after getting this information. I suddenly became weak because I knew this attack was meant to destroy my sister! ……

I sat on a chair back at home and tried to console myself with social media, but unfortunately for me the pictures of this widow had gone viral, I was successful in finding her on Facebook and stayed on her page for over 3 hours. As soon as I saw her, I was convinced she was a sister; pretty and graceful! Facebook informed me further, Barbara Mahama was a Jesus freak, she looked so cool when photographed and her smiles in the photos were so heartwarming. She was already impacting her community through Kindle Ghana Foundation. Now I burst into tears!

On my knees that night I asked God to rain on her strength "cats and dogs". The ensuing days were bleak and within two days my family, friends and colleagues knew that unless the conversation was about Barbara I was simply not interested!!!

On the 3rd of June I made a tough decision, I had a 4-minute video before me on Ghana web, I don't know why I did, but I looked at it and closed it after a minute, not out of fear, but my purpose for watching was accomplished. I could not sleep well after that, until 3 weeks later. Meanwhile I reported to work every day and got tired, but my mind and eyes refused to allow me rest.

As I stayed up those nights, I thought of this gentleman, who in this world at the point of death will refuse to defend himself especially with that type of pistol? (at this point I had even gone to the extent of reading on pistols).

Obviously, this was someone who valued souls even when these souls were extremely toxic! He calmly went home, because HIS WIFE had shown him the WAY HOME and left these toxic souls, so that they may have a chance of also being shown the way home someday. He may have never evangelized or mounted a crusade podium but he looked at these people who had failed to show him compassion with full compassion, PURE COMPASSION!! Compassion is a lost virtue and so for someone to depict such a virtue under that circumstance, it means that his heart was filled with CHRIST! OH!! Jesus certainly received this beautiful soul, not an angel because that is how he felt towards men when he walked here on earth. (Matthew 9:36).

I also added on to my prayer schedule, the salvation of the souls of these people that the devil had used because most certainly he had dumped them after using them. Anytime anyone of them will get to know the way HOME, Maxwell would jump for joy and an additional crown would be received. They were used as agents, they hurt us so bad! but the greatest payback to the devil is for him to lose their souls. And I know that, one day, at their last breath they would find their way home and will be eternally grateful to Maxwell. I'll keep praying for them. It will be great to see them worship with us before THE THRONE someday.

I also knew that Barbara, the wife was meant for a lot more. God knows all his girls and that Monday morning, fully aware of the plan of the devil even before time begun, He did not stop it. Hmmmm, He rather would use this to bring Barbara to the expected end. Barbara is not ordinary!! I kept telling everyone including those who didn't even want to hear. You're hearing about her or there is no conversation!

The date for the funeral was announced and it was going to be a State one. The intensity of the prayer had to be increased because my sister was to prove that 2 Cor 1:4 was pure truth, she had to show all including the powers and principalities that God is good no matter what. I was a certified mourner at this stage and my mother who was on leave at that time was my lieutenant.

On my way to the office that morning, I saw my newly found sister in front of the DAILY GRAPHIC! Wheew! The whole world was rather waiting to see her 'dramatize' her pain. I was not happy the picture was there, but I knew she was made for signs and wonders so there was no problem with the picture flying around. I told myself that her pictures would re-appear someday, but it would be because of exploits. I consoled myself with these thoughts.

Then my sister's public reaction....

My entrance to the office got my colleagues surprised; 'ah we thought you'd be at the state house?'. I did not mind them. My line manager gave me no files because he knew I was hot! Very hot! Then around 10am my mum called and said 'Maame, Barbara read two tributes! One for herself and one for the kids without shedding a tear! She even drew an applause from the crowd. Rushing quickly to the washroom, I looked into the mirror and said, WE ARE TRULY MORE THAN CONQUERORS!!!

Her anchor kept soul, steadfast and sure while the billows rolled,

The anchor was fastened to the ROCK WHICH CANNOT MOVE!

I praised God! Got the clip later and watched it several times. I was glad because everyone would know that strength was DIVINE. God was glorified, and that's what Daddy's girls live for! People attributed it to the help of the counsellors, men of God and psychologists but I attributed it to YOU BARBARA! You had filled your heart with the word of God and spent much time in His presence, so God's comfort was quite easy to receive. Many people have gone through lesser challenges; seen Men of God, psychologists and counsellors but remained same, but not YOU Barbara, not YOU!!

I saw on your Linked in profile that you had studied on Crisis Management. I want to only understand that course from a lay person's point of view, how you handled this pain was unfathomable. On a more serious note, University of Ghana has to give you honorary doctorate letters for that course! (That is if the content of the course means what I'm thinking anyway). Daddy was proud of you that day and I know you will always make Him proud!

If you were older, I may not have been interested in all these, but you are rather a God-fearing young lady who has the hunger to impact her world, a trail blazer and a generational changer! You are in my generation and most importantly a sister from another mother. (God is our Daddy) so I was also in this.

Devil, you targeted the wrong one!

Oh, you messed up big time!!

I would constantly repeat this in prayer!

I kept praying and as the days went by, the media coverage of you faded. Sometimes I would spend almost the whole day with your word press blog opened on my PC, waiting for an article. I just wanted to know how you were faring. I asked a lot of friends if they knew you personally but none of them were in your network.

Your article that Sunday morning made me glad that at least i had heard from you and even though you were crashed, you were not destroyed. That led to getting your e-mail address. I sent an email hoping for a reply, but everything was still fresh, so I honestly thought there would be no reply. But no! you replied and actually gave your phone number!

At your first reply to my message, all my friends and family around the globe were aware that I was finally in touch with BARBARA MAHAMA! They were all happy because of my attachment to the issue. You warmed up over time and made me comfortable enough to the extent that I could count on you for help with ….. In your pain, you reached out to pull her out of pain and overwhelmed by your love, she rededicated her life to Christ. There's definitely a crown awaiting you for that!

Why would I spend my Saturday, telling you this?

Firstly, Maxwell's reaction changed my life! I respect people more than I used to do. I chat with security men, cleaners, beggars on the street and all people I never really had time for. I realized that, if someone looked at a human being and saw something more powerful than physical appearance and even lost his life in respect to human life, then I had to change my ways. I normally would drive alone to work, knowing that there are colleagues on my route for the nonsense of 'being in the spirit'. I pick them up now, one of them within the short space of time has given his life to Christ as I spoke to him sometimes about the brevity of life. Yesterday, as I played one of my favourite songs; 'HE changed me and I will never be the same', he sang along with so much passion. All the hip-hop songs are now off his phone and replaced with spirit filled songs. He comes along with me to church now. Praise the Lord!

Barbara, this whole incident changed my life!

I love more now

I smile wider now

I hug tighter now

Because the brevity of life has been made real in my life and I live each day thinking about how I can make this world better than I met it by touching lives.

You have trained yourself and acquired some skills in women empowerment, maternal issues, children and most importantly, you are growing yourself in the love of GOD. With this tenacity you are building, nothing would stop you

Barbara! I feel so blessed to be in the same generation with you. You will not only become a voice in the kingdom but a GENERAL amongst women in Africa. You are soaring my sister, your wings cannot be broken by any strong tides. You are a mother eagle now, who would train many eaglets to stop walking among the chicks and fly!

The devil would still try some tricks, but victory belongs to Jesus!

Finally, I would like to say a big thank you to You for doing this for all of us; your sisters!

Thank you for not accepting pity.

Thank you for embracing the strength of the Lord.

Thank you for showing the world that strength can only be found in the Lord.

Thank you for showing us that, we can have a great impact on our husbands.

Thank you for teaching us that we can make our husbands' lives beautiful.

Thank you for teaching us that we can have a great family and still touch our world.

Thank you for teaching us that we can even grieve gracefully.

Thank you for teaching ME that we can touch other lives even when we are in pain.

I could never write such a long 'thing' but I have, because of you, so THANK YOU!

There's still so much that I would like to add up, but this is fine.

Isaiah 61: 3-8 (NLT)

To all who mourn in Israel,

he will give a crown of beauty for ashes,

a joyous blessing instead of mourning,

festive praise instead of despair.

In their righteousness, they will be like great oaks

that the Lord has planted for his own glory.

4 They will rebuild the ancient ruins,

repairing cities destroyed long ago.

They will revive them,

though they have been deserted for many generations.

5 Foreigners will be your servants.

They will feed your flocks

and plow your fields

and tend your vineyards.

6 You will be called priests of the Lord,

ministers of our God.

You will feed on the treasures of the nations

and boast in their riches.

7 Instead of shame and dishonor,

you will enjoy a double share of honor.

You will possess a double portion of prosperity in your land,

and everlasting joy will be yours.

8 "For I, the Lord, love justice.

I hate robbery and wrongdoing.

I will faithfully reward my people for their suffering

and make an everlasting covenant with them.

9 Their descendants will be recognized

and honored among the nations.

Everyone will realize that they are a people

the Lord has blessed."

The above scripture is forever your portion!!

I wrote this today because it's been exactly two months but your progress impressive.

You are stronger.

You are wiser and

You are better!!! YOU INSPIRE ME BARBARA, I LOVE YOU!

28th December, 2017

The year of Greatness and Divine Elevation!!!

As the clock ticked 2016 away, we all praised God and sang into the New Year. "This is the year of elevation!" My Bishop declared, and as "expressionful" as I am, I just burst into tears as I needed elevation in most areas of my life. As a universal Christian, I looked out for the theme of sister churches the next day. In Lighthouse, it was the year of Greatness and in ICGC too, it was the year of Leadership, so by 2nd January, I was too convinced that no matter how the year turns out, it was just going to be a great one!.......

On the other side, I believe Barbara too was doing more. She had to pray for her husband, kids, job etc. by attending Answer Time, Turning Point service, other half and all-night prayers. Resolutions and expectations were brought before the Lord. The scripture "the expectation of the righteous shall not be cut short" was the banner used in pushing for our requests.....

When I finished my exam in May, I felt very disturbed. I must say, one of the greatest gifts I have received in life is well-meaning friends. They reached out to me; surprise lunch outings, sending my favourite Kish and other items through courier and beautiful texts to reassure me of their love. I know some scriptures, but they just remained scriptures to me because my heart was too disturbed to feel God's peace. But thanks be to God, who uses bad situations to bring out good stuff!

On 30th May, this loneliness and lack of peace gave way to deep thinking about real life. I had no reason to be worried; I rather had to make good use of the gift of life. The gift of life is the greatest gift, and if I had it, there was no reason to worry, for a living dog is definitely better than a dead lion and to all the living, there is hope for a better tomorrow.

Barbara, this year has been no doubt the most difficult year for you, but in your turmoil, I found strength, hope and divine encouragement. I looked at you then and still look at you now to receive a certain disposition about life. There is this extreme peace I feel in my heart these days, and for your information, even though I still cry a lot, it is only when I'm thankful. You as a person would never understand how your composure between 30th May and 9th June; days for which you were the most important subject for discussion and media highlight in Ghana, impacted my life. On 31st December, TV stations will telecast the year in review and your picture or face will not be missing in action. For the rest of our lives and beyond, google and YouTube will have records of your show of resilience, because when the devil sought to destroy you, God turned it!!! And rather made you a celebrity!

Errrrm Barbara, So how were you able to pick up those "shades" to wear on that day?

And the way you sat there too! So well composed, no drama!!! How did you do it?

As for my elder sister, the way you even cat walked was her major highlight. Till now, I don't know how you did it. In fact, for me, the most surprising was your composure at the vigil; errrm, I followed that online too! There were no shades, so I could see your eyes, you showed great resilience that night sis, controlling so much pain at such a tender age. I could not believe that someone in her twenties, no matter her temperament in addition to counselling could do this. But thanks be to God who raised a prayer army on your behalf when you could barely whisper a prayer for yourself and the kids.

At least, I know how I labored in prayer on this subject, so I can answer myself and say that, God was in it. My effort was even less than 0.00001%, it is therefore not surprising that you didn't lose your mind, God was too much in it, so it had to work out!

As I saw your picture every morning, I consistently lost weight, by the time I saw your picture on Bishop Dag's visit,

I was sure by then both of us had suddenly dropped to size 10! However, 9th June gave me hope, because even though that was the day you were expected to be looking lost, pale and unable to co-ordinate your steps, you looked much better. When I saw you in the media, I concluded that you were someone who didn't really care about what people would say! I became happy because I knew that with such personality, you would get better with time. While others who lack understanding saw a platform for criticism, I saw a role model for my emotions.

The greatest act in that period to me, was the wording of your tribute. You mentioned little about how difficult life was going to be and even sought to let people look at life in a more meaningful way. What surprised me most was that you said nothing about the process of how he transitioned. At that point, I fell in love with you all over again after the initial one 11 days earlier! Still, those who lacked understanding thought it was not emotional enough. They expected words like "How will I survive without you?", "I will never get over this" with interlude of tears! I never understood that they just couldn't even be happy that at least you were strong!

It's fine, I'll manage…….

This is a statement you wrote in your tribute; it probably didn't mean much to people or it was a normal word you used. But that statement was my change agent.

You were going to manage what?

The pain?

The loneliness?

The emptiness or exactly what?

If a forty-year-old wrote this, it wouldn't be much of an issue for me. But a twenty-nine-year-old was ready to manage such pain! I believe that there are many shattered dreams, but you didn't focus on that, you were ready to manage and you really are managing!!! And now, I have really learnt how to manage too!.....

There is nothing more painful in life than broken dreams, which you suffered this year in greater measure, but looking at you now, I'm more convinced that there is even beauty in the brokenness of Daddy's girls. Because of broken dreams, I'm able to make so much time for others now, some have received my love and affection, my resources are people-oriented and many other good stuff! In learning to manage, I have become more peaceful, hopeful and trusting. The pain of broken dreams sometimes tries to show up, but hey! We are victorious!!! ......

Barbara, if there's any situation more than strenuous, hard, baffling, perplexing, mysterious, unfathomable, exhausting, tiring, back-breaking or painful that anyone could ever meet, then that's what 29th May of this year brought you. This was supposed to be Your Year of Greatness, so this is obviously not what you expected, but at this very moment, Barbara, you have become nothing less than GREAT!!! SO TODAY, Let's praise God some more, because even in this, He watched over His word and used the most unsuspecting situation to cause you to walk in your high places. The year is closing; this has been your most eventful year, a year filled with pain but greatness also and most importantly, new life lessons learnt. In the coming years, watch out well, all the themes declared will definitely impact your life......

Writing to tell you all the stuff I've learnt from you, while you are around to know how I feel about you gives me joy, because most of the time, we write about people when they can't read or hear it.

Getting in touch with you and everything else has been one of my highlights for 2017. It means a lot to me, because you helped me a lot!.....

I would like to say a big thank you AGAIN to You for doing this for all of us; your sisters!

Time Wasters

I have realised that during grieving moments, there are things that serve as time wasters. Attempts are made to solve little problems. The attempt is good, but if the attempt deprives a widow of sleep such that she has to miss work the following day or she has to go to work sleepy and tired, it is not in her best interest. Attempts made must not put the interest of others over others; all attempts must be fair to the parties involved. Anyone who serves as a mediator for these occasions should weigh the options and the end goal and put the well-being of the kids and their future before any other thing. Attempts that seek to put fear in widows and make them feel their lives are about to be miserable unless they are in subjection to other people's whims and caprices so they can be shielded is negative and must be discouraged.

Letters to Daddy

dear daddy

I make a promise to you that the whole world will know you and me and my mommy and brother will keep that promise. you meant the world to me he was the best daddy I loved the stuff you made for me and the presents you were so kind you never deserved that

i love you so much

Love from Jerry. ♥

From Jaden to Daddy
Daddy you are the best Daddy
ever you didn't deserve to die

Love from Jaden ♥

Some Words of Exhortation from the Bible

Psalms 34:18

The Lord is close to the brokenhearted and saves those who are crushed in spirit.

Don't ever think God is far from you while you go through your down moments. He is closer than you think, and he will comfort you. God cares for us. He loves us. Just believe.

Isaiah 43:19

Behold, I will do a new thing; now it shall spring forth; shall ye not know it? I will even make a way in the wilderness and rivers in the desert.

It is difficult to see the new thing God says he will do in your life when you lose someone very dear to you. He expects us to be like children and put our whole trust and belief in him.

Joshua 1:9

Have I not commanded you? Be strong and of good courage; do not be afraid, nor be dismayed, for the Lord your God is with you wherever you go.

Being strong and courageous is a command from God. He has given us assurance that He will be with us wherever we go.

Proverbs 3:5-6

Trust in the Lord with all your heart, and lean not on your own understanding; In all your ways acknowledge Him, and He shall direct your path.

Whatever situation you find yourself in, trust in Jehovah and lean on Him alone to direct you and bring you out of the situation gloriously.

Romans 8:28

And we know that all things work together for good to those who love God, to those who are called according to His purpose.

All means all, the good and the bad will work together for your good as a child of God. The devil may think he has won in the beginning, but God will always come through. Just believe.

I leave you with these words:

- There is power in the name of Jesus Christ, and the blood of Jesus is efficient, and it speaks better things for us.

- There is a God who rules in the affairs of men; believe in Him fully.

- When God chooses you, He has chosen you.

- Showing kindness, loving, and doing good are all virtues God puts in His chosen. If you find yourself doing these, God is with you. If you find yourself finding it difficult to love, to show kindness, to speak good into people's lives, ask God to fill you with these virtues, and the Holy Spirit will help you. We are in this world to help humanity.

Forever in our hearts Maxwell. We will always love you!-

B.